PIERLUIGI ROMEO DI COLLOREDO MELS

FROM SIDI EL BARRANI TO BEDA FOMM 1940- 1941

OPERATION COMPASS: AN ITALIAN PERSPECTIVE.

THE AUTHOR

Count Pierluigi Romeo di Colloredo Mels was born in Rome in 1966.
Archaeologist and military historian, he is author of numerous works on the history of the two world wars and the Italian interwar conflicts, Ethiopia and Spain, and of the units of the MVSN, the subject of which he is considered one of the leading international experts. Among his latest works, *Camicia Nera! Storia delle unità combattenti della Milizia Volontaria Sicurezza Nazionale dalle origini al 25 luglio*, *Südfront. Il Feldmaresciallo Albert Kesselring nella campagna d'Italia 1943- 1945*; *Da Sidi el Barrani a Beda Fomm 1940- 1941* (here translate in English); *Per vincere ci vogliono i leoni... I fronti dimenticati delle camicie nere, 1939- 1940*; *Controguerriglia! La 2ª Armata italiana e l'occupazione dei Balcani 1941- 1943*; *Confine orientale. Italiani e slavi sull'Amarissimo dal Risorgimento all'esodo*; *Giugno 1940. La battaglia delle Alpi.* Colloredo is also editor of *Storia Rivista* and collaborates with the magazines *Nova Historica, Storia in Rete, Ritterkreuz, Fronti di guerra* and *Il Primato Nazionale*.
He is a former Officier of the 3rd *Granatieri "Guardie"* Regiment

STORIA

ISBN: 9788893276672 prima edizione Novembre 2020
SPS-049 EN - FROM SIDI EL BARRANI TO BEDA FOMM 1940- 1941 by Pierluigi Romeo di Colloredo Mels
Editor: **Luca Stefano Cristini Editore per i tipi di Soldiershop serie Storia-** Cover & Art Design: L. S. Cristini e P. Romeo di Colloredo Mels

SUMMARY:

Preface pag. 5

June 1940: Italo Balbo's death and the early stages of the war. Pag. 7

The Forces on Field Pag. 13

Operazione E: the Italian advance on Sidi el Barrani Pag. 27

Operation *Comass*: Wavell's offensive. Pag. 39

The fall of Bardia Pag. 47

Fox killed in the open: the battle of Beda Fomm Pag. 55

Graziani leaves, Rommel arrives Pag. 59

Conclusion Pag. 63

Chronology Pag. 71

The conquest of Sidi el Barrani. Marshal Graziani's Relation to the *Comando Supremo*, 18 September 1940. Pag. 129

Operation *Compass* in the bulletins of the Italian Comando Supremo Pag. 131

Operations in Libya. Wawell's Report to the War Cabinet in London, February 1941 Pag. 141

Italian tanks' technical data Pag. 143

Bibliography Pag. 147

The arch of the Fileni, built by Italo Balbo on the border between Tripolitania and Cyrenaica (drawing by Kurt Caesar, 1941. Author's collection).

PREFACE

But what is wrong with this army if five Divisions manage to be pulverized in two days?

(Galeazzo Ciano, *Diary*, 11 December 1940).

The defeat suffered in Egypt and Cyrenaica by the troops of Marshal Rodolfo Graziani, which culminated in the annihilation of the 10th Army at Beda Fomm in February 1941, constitutes the most serious defeat of the Italian army in the course of its history, even worse than that which took place on October 24, 1917 in the basin of Plezzo and in Tolmin it went down in history with the name of *la battaglia di Caporetto*. But as for Caporetto, the *Regio Esercito*, far from being defeated, recovered immediately also and above all thanks to the help of the Third Reich and to the example provided by the *Deutsches Afrika Korps* units.
After Caporetto come the Piave, and after Sidi el Barrani, Bardia and Beda Fomm come Bir el Gobi, Tobruk and Gazala.
However, for Italy the defeat in Cyrenaica was a severe downsizing and the end of the parallel war, with strategic subordination to the German Reich.
The initial campaign of the Italo-British conflict in North Africa has been overshadowed in Italy - where the defeat of Graziani was to be overshadowed in light of the far superior performance of Italian soldiers, even in situations of inferiority- in the United Kingdom by subsequent events and by the myth of Rommel; and apart from some notable exceptions, the works on the subject are affected by a remarkable chauvinism: often in the bibliographies of so much British historiography only and only British sources are indicated, obviously biased, often veiledly racist and reflective the war propaganda that saw the Italians as pompous and arrogant cowards. always ready to raise their hands, and the same happens in the Italian one which oscillates between justifying the defeat and attributing it to the guilt of Mussolini or Graziani and of a real or presumed Italian war unpreparedness.
We will analyze both the military and political aspects of the campaign, without necessarily wanting to make personal judgments, which we also think are evident from the same exposition of the narrated facts.
Caporetto, we said. And there were in fact episodes that recalled the unfortunate autumn of 1917, not only for the presence of Italian colonists refugees from Cyrenaica, but also for the spread of panic and the collapse of morale.
Mario Tobino remembers in *Il deserto della Libia*:

> (Undated.) - The ambulances that came from Cyrenaica after the abandonment, were studded with red crosses, with international health flags; above the roof another huge red cross.
> They were led by a brown man with very healthy people who were afraid. They arrived in Tripoli at all hours, in those three days of arrival of the fugitives; and the ambulance flags, those eyes and faces that could be seen inside, those dusty and slapped caissons, told the story of the twenty years.
> These people, after they had descended on the safe ground of Tripoli, did not stop being afraid, and thought of other escape plans. The negro had now freed himself and screamed in them without restraint. The trembling lips, those gestures of a drama co-

median, those voices that told non-existent descriptions. The word was always heard: run away.
(Then, when the Germans began to disembark, all the Negroes immediately became heroes again. A few seconds after the arrival of the Germans they immediately forgot about the escape; but in dreams, every night it reappeared.)
The heroes, the flags, the fumes, the cackles arrived. They had one thousand two hundred kilometers on their legs.
I was in Tripoli. At the last stage. As soon as they arrived they asked for the road to Tunisia.
Escape is a pleasure, they wanted to continue it. It seemed they wanted to escape all their lives.
And many came to the hospital.
I was a doctor from the Bu-sect, from the Tripoli military hospital. I saw ambulances crammed with aviators, who, they told me, had fled Cyrenaica to Tripoli, in an ambulance, that is, by land, and not on the airplanes, which were still there, because flying was dangerous.
English hunting was faster, he could have reached and killed them, while instead escaping in ambulances, with red crosses painted, it was safer.
And so the few others arrived, because the so-called "fugone" did so in a few.
Soldiers who were wounded in the head were seen, because their heads had been beaten foggyly by mounting on the fleeing truck, in fact to escape there was the fight for the place on the trucks. And then once up, away, for hundreds and hundreds of kilometers. And when they arrived in Tripoli they didn't want to stop. It was to be believed that the mists were swept once and for all, once that fear had passed; now they would begin to see reality, and their reality, with clean eyes. Instead it was not so. In the meantime, therefore,in Tripoli all those, few, who had managed to escape the encirclement, few because the majority were regularly encircled and the different tried nothing to escape the English encirclement because they were happy to become prisoners and finally stop with the desert, of which they were very tired , and since they were equally tired of that confusion that they did not understand well what and why there was, but which they also felt existed.

It is difficult to judge how an army of 150,000 men could have left 133,298 prisoners, 420 tanks, 845 cannons and 564 airplanes in the hands of a strong enemy of 36,000 in the space of exactly two months, from 9 December 1940 to 9 February 1941, undergoing its strategic initiative and moral superiority, especially in light of the far better performances of the *Regio Esercito* from March 1941 to May 1943 with armaments gradually more and more dated in the face of an opponent that is on the contrary stronger and stronger.
*From Sidi el Barrani to Beda Fomm h*as the objective to present a wiew of Wawell's *whirlwind victory* from the other side of the hill. The Italian perspective.

JUNE 1940:
BALBO'S DEATH AND THE EARLY STAGES OF THE WAR.

At the outbreak of the war the Italians in Libya had to face the French forces of Tunisia and the British forces of Egypt; but after the armistice of Villa Incisa in Olgiata between Italy and France, French troops in Tunisia and Algeria were demobilized. The western sector was losing importance and Italo Balbo, Air Marshal and Governor of Libya, was able to concentrate the best troops at his disposal in the Cyrenaean sector, also because during the first week of the war British troops had penetrated across the border capturing some Italian officers located in isolated areas.
On June 20 Italo Balbo telegraphed the following dispatch to Badoglio:

> Dear Badoglio, you are perfectly aware of our situation in eastern Libya and I don't need to spend a word to illustrate it: our assault tanks, now old and armed only with machine guns, are largely outdated; the machine guns of the British armored cars riddles them with shots, happily passing the armor; we do not have armored cars; anti-tank means, for the most part fallback; modern ones generally lack the proper ammunition.
> So the fight takes on the character of the meat against the iron, which also explains some episodes too well, fortunately of little importance.
> I have informed you of the measures taken; I have stripped the 5th Army of troops and vehicles and the situation is improving. Now that the war in France is coming to an end, would it be possible to get fifty of their magnificent tanks and armored personnel carriers from the Germans for Libya? It would be the steel point of the offensive we want to conduct against Egypt. This offensive of ours could develop simultaneously with the attack on England; the Libyan - Egyptian front is the only one in the world where the British can be attacked directly, on a first-order target - the Suez Canal - and the sure overwhelming success, when we had some armored and armored vehicles, would have first-rate material and moral significance. Show this letter to the Duce.

Obviously, the request for German tanks and armored cars remained a dead letter. However, the tactical situation of Italian North Africa remained serious due to the lack of supplies from Italy. Moreover, Balbo himself had told the *Duce* on 11 May that

> With the increase of 80,000 men, the proportion between the troops under my orders and the adversaries will be one by two [Balbo also considered the French troops, editor's note], but this is of little importance: it is not the number of enemies that make me worries, but their armament. Today the most fair legion of Caesar would succumb to a section of machine guns.

Moreover, the British began to torment the Italian border garrisons with raids of Rolls Ryce armored cars: thus in the first days of the war the elimination of the garrison of the Reduced Capuzzo occurred on June 14, the capture of General Lastrucci, commander of the Engineer Corps of the 10th Army and, more serious, the annihilation of the D'Avanzo Column on 16 June. Certainly these actions must be evaluated as pinpricks in the Italian device, yet it was these pinpricks that highlighted a whole series of shortcomings of the Italian military apparatus in Cyrenaica, as well as causing a lowering of morale.

The harbour of Tripoli
(Kurt Caesar, 1941. author's collection)

The first border clashes lend themselves to a series of considerations on Italian forces. The troops fought tenaciously against the raiders, and the cause of their reverses lay in the general lack of vehicles in the Italian device, which made the application of a mobile defense difficult and forced the Italians to remain anchored to a static defense for single cornerstones that were punctually overwhelmed by motorized forces.

The numerical advantage of the Italians was therefore nullified by the greater mobility of the British forces which managed to obtain from time to time a local superiority against the various Italian cornerstones; the comparison between armored vehicles was also against the Italians: the destruction of the Avanzo column is the most striking example. The Italians were equipped, in that case, with L3 tanks (CV33), armed with two 8mm machine guns and weakly protected, while the British had perhaps not excellent tanks, like the A9 *Cruisers*, but certainly more armed.

Marshal Balbo immediately began to take steps to stem the British initiative by moving troops and materials from Tripolitana to Cyrenaica.

In a telegram directed to the General Staff, Balbo downsized the successes of the British patrols across the Libyan border:

> I see an English and French bulletin that tells cheerful lies constantly. I collect in this moment beautiful episode. Pilots of our tanks riddled with armored machine guns, though dying, still defended themselves. I remember a small episode of the Esc Schegga garrison that resisted for three days although surrounded. It is such fear that these soldiers of ours and enemy barbarism inspire that English, instead of collecting seriously injured officers in our tanks, finished them with hand grenades. However first phase of surprise is overcome. If we do not want the English bulletins to continue on an increasingly bold tone, our bulletins will have to be more eloquent.

The cause before this situation must undoubtedly be considered the first orders issued by Badoglio, and the lack of initiative that ensued to facilitate the British raids on the Cyrenaic border, with the consequent demoralization of troops and commands, already worried by information alarms of the S.I.M. which gave the enemy forces more consistent and dangerous than the real, ideas against which Balbo attempted to fight also from the point of view of morale, showing that the British raiders were not invulnerable, and going to personally capture an armored car on June 21 in Bir el Gobi: after sighting the armored personnel carrier Rolls Royce m.24 during a mission with his SM79 avBalbo immediately fell to the ground while the second pilot Ottavio Frailich immediately took off again flying over the armored vehicle, then captured by the ground troops coordinated by the same Marshal of the Air.

It is now established that on the Egyptian front our numerical superiority over the British was 5 to 1, even if the tactical and logistical organization and the training of the troops left a lot to be desired compared to the adversaries. The Royal Air Force and the Royal Navy were also more modern and powerful than their opponents.

On the twenty-eighth of June 1940 the plane on which Balbo was traveling was hit by fire from the Italian anti-aircraft gun of the port of Tobruk.

Balbo that fatal June 28 flew from Derna to reach the camp of Tobruk. The formation consisted of two *Savoia Marchetti* SM 79s, one piloted by Balbo and the other, who was saved, by Major Felice Porro.

On board the plane of Balbo were Major Ottavio Frailich, captain Gino Cappannini, marshal Giuseppe Berti. In addition to the crew, Major Claudio Brunelli, Lieutenant

Count Cino Florio and Lino Balbo, Console of the Fascist Militia Enrico Caretti and the aforementioned Captain Nello Quilici were also on board.

Around 5.30 pm, near the Tobruk airport, Balbo saw two columns of smoke due to an English bombing that took place a few minutes earlier. He gave the order to land but without warning on the ground.

The Air Marshal's SM79 was exchanged both by the anti-aircraft on the ground, and by the cruiser *San Giorgio*, and by the submarine *Marcantonio Bragadin*, for one of the British planes that had carried out the bombing, and hit. According to some, the deadly burst was fired not by criuser *San Giorgio* but by the submarine's turret, which later left quickly.

> Anti-aircraft batteries fill the sky as soon as it is calm again over Tobruk. The 100/47mm guns of the San Giorgio project buckets of shrapnel, the Breda machine guns from the anti-aircraft emplacements all around the port shoot tracers madly. They are all headed for the defenseless and lonely three-engine plane approaching in peace and having no radio on board. They don't take it. Nobody on board notices initially, but then lowering on the track the shots get closer, the target becomes clear. The blows reach him. The engines are engulfed in flames, the wings are torn and the fireball crashes to the ground without leaving survivors. Italo Balbo is dead.

The dismay in Italy and in the colonies was enormous: national mourning was declared and Balbo and his comrades were led in a procession to Benghazi and then to Tripoli, where he was buried and where he remained until 1970, the year in which, following the advent in Gaddafi's power, the remains were moved to Italy and taken to Orbetello, where Balbo still rests.

He was succeeded by the best known of the colonial generals; Marshal of Italy Rodolfo Graziani.

When Marshal Graziani landed in Castel Benito, Tripoli airport, he immediately set to work to report the deficiencies he found in Libya to his superiors.

Under the leadership of Graziani, in the summer of 1940 the Italians organized light self-armed forces through which they gradually retrenched the aggressiveness of the British. Meanwhile, the 10th Army began preparations for an offensive in Egypt.

Graziani had been ordered to attack Egypt on July 15th. Balbo had died on June 28th and already June 29th the Marshal of Italy was already on the "fourth bank"; the times for an offensive were very tight. The Italian attack on the British posts was made necessary, as Badoglio had written to Balbo on the twenty-sixth of June 1940, because we do not want to remain at the conclusion of peace with empty hands.

Germany controlled all central-western Europe directly or indirectly, and after the French defeat, the German Divisions were concentrating in the Calais area of northern France for the *Seelöwe* operation. The invasion of England seemed something resolved in a few weeks for the forces of the Third Reich. Mussolini therefore deemed it appropriate to attack in Egypt, the only Great Britain's "land" front.

Political reasons prevailed over other military ones.

When Graziani asked the Chief of Staff of Balbo, General Giuseppe Tellera, what the Air Marshal's plans were for an offensive against Egypt, he replied that there was no real plan:

> These were only ideas that Marshal Balbo had - Graziani will report - however never precisely specified. In any case, according to Tellera, they cannot be implemented due to

the lack of adequate means.

On the days of July 2 and 3 Marshal Graziani represented the situation of the land and air armed forces, as well as the indispensable needs of the means previously requested by Air Marshal Balbo.
It is interesting to reproduce telegrams 17, 18 and 19 sent by Graziani to Marshal Badoglio.

> Ranked # 17. Available forces North Africa are now divided into two blocks.
> A western one that includes XX and X armed corps (5th Army) with the following Divisions: *Pavia, Brescia, Sirte, Savona, Bologna, Sabratha*, 2 CC.NN.
> - Total mass seven Divisions.
> Having sold all vehicles to the eastern mass, they are not self-transportable.
> Their transport from Tripoli to East Benghazi undermined by English submarines crossing in that sea.
> Eastern block (10th Army) east consisting of Army Corps XXI, XXII, XXIII, with the following Divisions:
> I CC.NN[1]. - *Cirene* - *Catanzaro* - IV CC.NN. - I *Libya* - II *Libya – Marmarica*.
> Total seven Divisions.
> Between Misda, Naluth, Zuara and around Tripoli there are seven Libyan battalions among veterans and newly established.
> I have ordered a meeting in Agedabia with air transport which will immediately begin to protect any communication threat between Tripolitania and Cyrenaica and with further tasks that I reserve the right to specify and communicate.
> At East Benghazi indigenous battalion paratroopers force 250 ready to use. At Misurata est sends national paratroopers battalion forces about three hundred volunteers. I ordered a transfer to Barce.
> Two hundred parachutes are missing, of which an request has been made and please send them.

> Ranked # 18. From the five telegrams relating to the ground forces situation and due to the need for their movement and maneuver, it is imperative to send the following vehicles already requested by Maresciallo Balbo: a thousand vehicles, the maximum possible number of tankers as well as tanks and other means of water transport, maximum quantities of fuel. No further sending of men is required except for specialized ones.

> Ranked # 19. Air vehicle situation. Existing equipment initially 315. Lost 60. In agreement with the Air Force Superior Command, consider it more profitable that instead of units, the necessary complements are sent from Italy to complete staff and make up for losses.

After receiving these telegrams, Marshal Badoglio sent the following telegram to the Commander General of the Armed Forces in Libya on July 3 (available in the Historical Diary of the *Comando Supremo*):

> 1067. July 3. 09.15 am. For Marshal Graziani - Duce orders me to inform you that it is vital interest for Italy that you are ready to launch offensive for day 15 (fifteen) to be synchronous with action - German. Having to rely essentially on existing materials in the colony. Telegraphed for absolutely essential materials that we will send together me-

---

[1] CCNN: *Camicie Nere*, National Fascist Party's Black Shirts

dium tanks in convoy. You know our availability and our difficulties. You have happily overcome Somalia enormous difficulties - you will overcome them now - Give me assurances. Badoglio.

After receiving this telegram, Graziani asked all the high-ranking officers present in Libya to get a clear idea of the general situation of the Italian troops. Immediately afterwards he telegraphed again to Badoglio

Your reference 1067. 3 current and mine 21.
I communicate on day 15 I will start movement across the border with occupation Sollum - Halfaia. Means currently available do not allow me further immediate outreach. My intention is to make the first detachment to enter enemy territory and remove enemy pressure from our frontier. I will then measure further possibilities. Please confirm the starting date keeping in mind that tanks will arrive only in Tobruk tomorrow evening and after tomorrow 14 at the foot of the work.
Graziani.

Marshal Badoglio replied with telegram nr. 1274 of 13 July:

The starting date of the operations had been indicated by me in principle. You will begin operations when you deem it appropriate. In conclusion, you have complete freedom of action.
Badoglio.

After a few hours another Badoglio telegram arrived on Graziani's desk:

1299. *Duce* authorizes you to delay this operation until you have all the means that will allow you to perform a maneuver at a wide range and in depth in order to achieve results of considerable importance. Conquering Sollum and then stopping is not a profitable maneuver and therefore not to be carried out. I will let you know exactly when you can receive the materials agreed between your steward and the Army Superior Command. Mark me receipt
- Badoglio.

THE FORCES ON FIELD

The situation in Libya on the eve of Graziani's advance in Egypt in September 1940 was the following.
At the Tunisian border facing the defenses of the French Mareth line (the socalled *Maginot d'Afrique*) there was the 5th Army (General Italo Gariboldi), while at the border with Egypt was deployed the 10th Army (General Mario Berti).

The **5th Army** framed:

X *Corpo d'Armata* (General Alberto Barbieri):

Divisions

-25a *Bologna*:
39°-40° fanteria *Bologna*, 205° Artiglieria;

-55a *Savona*:
15°- 16° fanteria *Savona*, 12° Artiglieria *Sila*;

-60a *Sabratha*:
85°- 86° fanteria *Verona*, 42° Artiglieria *Sabratha*;

XX *Corpo d'Armata* (General Ferdinando Cona):

Divisions

-17a *Pavia*:
27°- 28° fanteria *Pavia*, 26° Artiglieria *Rubicone*;

-27a *Brescia*:
19°- 20° fanteria *Brescia*, 55° Artiglieria;

-61a *Sirte*:
69°- 70° fanteria *Ancona*, 43° Artiglieria *Sirte*;

XXIII *Corpo d'Armata* (General Annibale Bergonzoli):

Divisions

-1a CCNN *23 Marzo* (Fascist Militia):
219a - 233a Legione, 201° Artiglieria;

-2a CCNN *28 Ottobre* (Fascist Militia):
231a -238a Legione, 202° Artiglieria;

-2ª *Libica*:
III- IV Raggruppamento Libico,
II Raggruppamento Artiglieria Libico;

The **10th Army,** in turn, framed:

XXI Corpo d'Armata (General Sebastiano Gallina):

Divisions

-62ª *Marmarica*:
115°- 116° fanteria *Treviso*, 44 Artiglieria *Marmarica*;

-63ª *Cirene:*
157°- 158° fanteria *Liguria*, 45° Artiglieria *Cirene;*

XXII Corpo d'Armata (General Pitassi Mannella):

Divisions

-64ª *Catanzaro*:
141°- 142° fanteria *Catanzaro*, 203° Artiglieria ;

-4ª CCNN *3 Gennaio* (Fascist Militia):
250ª -270ª Legione, 204° Artiglieria;

-1ª *Libica*:
III- IV *Raggruppamento Libico*, II *Raggruppamento Artiglieria Libico*;

In addition there were the *Truppe del Sahara Libico, Troops of the Libyan Sahara.*
The paper strength of an Italian metropolitan infantry division was two regiments of three battalions each of infantry, a machine gun battalion, and three battalions of artillery with a total of twenty-four 75/27mm field guns and twelve 100/17mm howitzers. A total of 11,000 men were in a division, with about 400 trucks and tractors, though after 1941 most infantry divisions usually numbered about 7,000 men in the field. With the exception of the German mountain division, Italy was the only great power to field a two-regiment division. This formation grew out of war experiences with Ethiopia, where a pair of two-regiment divisions operated successfully, moving quickly on that theater's poor road net, while deploying full divisional level artillery. Such a unit could have advantages in the rough terrain of Italy's mountainous European borders. The concept of this so-called "binary" division was that one division would fix an enemy division in place, allowing a second binary division to hit the fixed enemy unit in the flank. Part of the weakness of this organization was that the Italian infantry division in North Africa was never at full strength.
The Italian Divisions were division only in name:formed of binary regiments, they were practically brigades with an aggregate artillery regiment, while the British Divisions

a *Caproni Ghibli* CA 309 faces alone six British *supermarine spitfires* mk v b
(Kurt Caesar, 1941. author's collection)

had ternary regiments, and therefore had an additional Regiment.
One more Regiment meant having more force in arms and men than one less Regiment. The Italian Divisions were yes more numerous than the English imperial ones but they had a lower numerical consistency (considering the single Divisions). Adding armored vehicles, anti-tank rifles, anti-aircraft guns, mortars, trucks, it can be clearly understood that an Italian Division was much weaker than a similar British unit.
The reputation gained by the fascist regime with the conquest of the Empire and with the victory in Spain, however, had produced a considerable weakening of the Italian armed forces depapeurate in means and personnel, which in the short term could not have sustained yet another war effort at European level.

The commitments sustained by Italy had also contributed to modernizing, developing and testing new military techniques. In fact, precisely during the commitment of the Volunteer Troop Corps in Spain - where Mario Berti and Annibale Bergonzoli had fought - the concept of rapid-going war developed, at least theoretically, consisting of a set of operations based on the rapid movement of forces motorized, which was thus opposed to the war of position that had instead characterized the Great War.

The reform was initiated and entrusted to General Pariani, Undersecretary of State to the Ministry of War from 1936 to 1939, who undertook to initiate a change in the *Regio Esercito*, aimed at its modernization.

This effort materialized in the so-called Pariani Reform launched in 1938, with which the ternary Divisions were replaced with binary ones.

The "old" ternary Divisions were so called because they were based on three infantry and one artillery regiments, the latter articulated in turn on four groups, while the new binary Divisions were organized on two infantry regiments and one of artillery, articulated in turn into three groups. All this translated into a lightening of the units which would thus have been more agile and maneuverable. However, if the Italian commands on the one hand could have fast forces on the field from the other, they found themselves having to maneuver with numerically lower and therefore weaker Divisions, with a consequent lower ability to engage the enemy.

But this aspect went into the background as the reform met the consensus of many senior officers who saw in the new structure not a greater effectiveness of the army but rather a chance to make a career: in fact with the increase in the number of Divisions it would also have increased that of the generals of Division, a title coveted by many and which conferred a certain prestige. Finally, the regime also proved to be short-sighted: by supporting the reform, it was concerned only with being able to count, at least nominally, on a greater number of Divisions that would serve to increase the prestige on the domestic and international level of Italy.

Focusing on the numerical data, we can say that the new binary Divisions that were created after the Pariani reform could count approximately 13,500 men, in whose ranks it was expected that a Black Shirt assault legion divided into two battalions would also be framed, about 1,300 men to replace the third Regiment, to remedy - but only partially - the weakening in terms of infantry.

So, after the adoption of the binary infantry Division of the Pariani Order, it was decided to permanently assign two battalions of Black Shirts gathered in a legion. of Assault Black Shirts, together with autonomous machine gun companies and 45 mm mortars. binary Divisions.

This also served to silence the criticisms of the conservatives regarding the elimination of the divisional reserve (the third infantry Regiment), in view of the conception that that the logic of the binary Division was in the assignment of the tactical maneuver to the Army Corps rather than to the Division , and in the rebalancing (unfortunately not yet sufficient) between too large infantry and too little fire support.

It would not have been enough, and the inadequacy of the Italian binary Division - but in Libya the infantry Divisions had not even assigned the Black Shirt Assault legion! - compared to the British counterpart it would have appeared dramatically on the occasion of Wavell's counter-offensive, as we will see.

First inspections of the Italian troops in Libya revealed shortcomings involving *slovenly uniforms, mess halls, latrines, to inadequate medical supervision of local prostitutes.*

The poor training of the Italian troops in 1940 was such that Marshal Italo Balbo, Libyan commander at the start of the war, stated that he would have "to paint his plane red" to avoid being hit by friendly fire: it happened really at Tobruk on 28 june, 1940. Part of this was due to the lack of first rate Italian troops in the theater.
As Greene and Massignati wrote on their excellent work on North Africa's campaign,

> There is a theory that most of the combat in World War II was performed by the "elite" units, while the "regular" units simply did not measure up to the same degree. While some regular units like the United States 1st Infantry Division (The Big Red One), would have this elite status, it usually applied to the paratroops, armor, and similar units. The Italian army's successes and failures in World War II reflect this theory quite well.
> The Italian elite was composed of seasoned units, such as the *Bersaglieri* (sharpshooters, comparable to the *Jaegers* in the earlier European monarchial armies), *Alpini* or mountain, armor, artillery, and paratroop units. In the 1940 fighting in Egypt and Libya, not one of the twelve regiments of *Bersaglieri* were initially present, though they would be some of the first reinforcements to be rushed over from Italy[2]. Later, the *Folgore* paratroop division, really a brigade strength unit when assigned to Africa, would become famous during the fighting at El Alamein. Many units of Italy's army would fight well in the course of the war, even with inferior weapons, and, in some cases, poor leadership, but most of Italy's military successes in World War II are associated with these better units[3].

As regards the armored component, in northern Africa the Italians could have seven L tank battalions, one of which (IXth) with reduced personnel.
To these was added, on 7 July, the Command of the 4th Tank Infantry Regiment (*Fanteria Carrista*) on two battalions M 11/39 medium tanks, landed in Tripolitania between 6 and 7 July.
On July 7, the 10th Army therefore framed:

- IX Btg Carri L with 29 tanks (of the original 46 tanks, 17 had been lost in combat);
- XXI Btg Carri L with 46 tanks;
- LXII Btg Carri L with 46 tanks - assigned to the *Marmarica* Division;
- LXIII Btg Carri L with 46 tanks - assigned to the *Cirene* Division,

for a total of 138 CV33 light tanks.
Also reinforcing were:

a) had by the 5th Army:
- XX Btg. Carri L (50) to the 1st Libyan Division
- LXI Btg Carri L (46) to the 2nd Libyan Division, + 14, + 14;

b) arriving from Italy

- 4th Rgt.*Fanteria Carrista* (70 [but 72] M 11/39 tanks).

The number of Italian tanks was, on paper, remarkable. The reality was different. The

---

[2] The 10th Regiment, who fought at Beda Fomm in 1941.
[3] J. Greene, A. Massignani, *Rommel's North Africa Campaign*, New York 1994, p. 19.

Italians had superiority in number but not in quality. The L 3 (or CV33) tank was so called because it weighed only 3 tons - L stands for light - and was armed only with a twin 8mm machine gun.

The Libyan troops of the Royal Libyan Troop Corps (*Regio Corpo Truppe Libiche*) intended to be employed in the offensive in Egypt, were organized into two Divisions, the 1st Libyan Division (*Divisione Libica*, General Luigi Sibille) and the 2nd (Gen. Armando Pescatori) were classified in the XXI *Corpo d'Armata* (or Libyan Army Corps) under the command of General Sebastiano Gallina; they deserve a few words, having often been neglected by historiography. They were not real colonial troops, being more trained and, after the granting of Italian citizenship to the Libyans by Balbo in 1939 with the Royal Decree of 9 January, they were now considered metropolitan troops, with the stars worn on the collar. Furthermore, many Libyan ascari were veterans of the Italo-Ethiopian conflict, during which they had provided good evidence of themselves under Graziani's orders on the Somali front.

Unlike Eritrean and Somali troops, organized in independent battalions, the Libyans had the Regiment as their basic unit.

Particularly trained and combative - and the Australians would have seen him in Derna- was the Libyan Air Infantry (*Fanti dell'Aria*) Battalion,then 1st Libyan Paratrooper Regiment, out of two battalions, 1st *Nero* (*Black*), Libyan, surnamed the *Black Devils*, and 2nd *Paracadutisti Nazionali della Libia* (*National Paratroopers of Libya*, Italians) by Lieutenant Colonel Goffredo Tonini, an officer decorated with the Gold Medal for Military Valor, the first Italian paratrooper department, created in Castel Benito in 1938 by order of Marshal Italo Balbo.

Taking into account the increasing difficulties in the international scene, four CCNN divisions, the so called *libiche* (*Libyan*) were deployed in North Africa with the names: *23 Marzo*, *28 Ottobre*, *21 Aprile* and *3 Gennaio*. Mobilized in September 1939, they were regrouped immediately in two CCNN corps, the XXII CCNN corps and XXIII CCNN corps, under command of Generals Umberto Somma and Mario Berti respectively. Mario Berti would later command the Italian army defeated at Sidi Barrani in December of 1940 at the start of General O'Connor's offensive.

In a short time however the *21 Aprile* division was disbanded in order to reinforce the other three divisions and to replace elements of the infantry division *Catanzaro* sent to Africa. The *Cantanzaro* would fill itself out with Italians already in Africa by late fall of 1940. At the outset the four CCNN divisions included eight legions for a total of 24 CCNN battalions and four machine gun battalions, while the army supplied the engineers, services and artillery units. At the end of 1940 the MVSN had become a bulky and complex organization, able to deploy 312,000 men. Of these, 112,000 were in 194 active battalions (24 *Libyan* battalions, eight colonial battalions, 10 frontier battalions, 108 assault and mountain battalions, 39 replacement battalions, four Libyan machine gun battalions and one machine gun battalion). Additionally there were 64,000 men in 135 territorial battalions, 85,000 men in the MACA (Antiaircraft Militia), 25,000 in the MILMART (Maritime Militia).

The *Regia Aeronautica* in Libya deployed the 5th *Squadra Aerea* led by General Felice Porro. I. Italian warplanes tended to be under gunned compared to German or Commonwealth aircraft, though usually quite maneuverable and reasonably fast. Her bombers carried small bombloads and were never numerous. The Italians did not maintain their aircraft at the same operational level as did the Commonwealth, and they lacked

spare parts. It should be noted that their fighters lacked radios until well into the war.
In the notes of the Historical Diary of the Supreme Command, reference is made to a particular function for the air force in Libya: the anti-tank function.
The troops of the Royal Army did not have sufficient efficient cannons against medium and heavy enemy tanks and did not even have piercing bullets.
The only solution found by the high command of Rome was to give directives to the air squadrons stationed in Libya to cooperate profitably with the land forces in anti-tank function. Easier said that done...
For example, on June 28, 1940, a few hours before his shot down, Balbo telegraphed to Felice Porro, commander of the 5th Air Team:

> The use of aviation in the last few days is completely wrong. Planes should not be sent to attack armored personnel carriers if they are not in a group of more than twenty. Isolated armored personnel carriers must be driven out of the army's auto-columns.
> Move a remark to the command of the east sector to have too easily adhered to the demands of the army. Everyone does their job if you want aviation to be efficient when needed.

The telegram was duplicated and also sent to the Undersecretary of State for the Air Force General Pricolo, who sent a telegram to Marhal Badoglio on 8 July 1940 in which he sent the following message:

> I present to you, Excellency, a copy of the letter signed by the late *Marshal* Balbo, relating to the use of the Air Force on the Cyrenaic front at the request of the X Army Command. I fully agree with what is expressed in the aforementioned letter as this use is to be considered, completely erroneous, scarcely effective and absolutely not in line with the characteristics of the vehicles. The spirit of collaboration of the Air Force, already so widely demonstrated on every occasion, must not justify requests that are in contrast with the most basic methods of use of the air departments.
> The devices supplied could not be considered ideal in any aspect. The bombers were SM 81 notoriously overtaken for speed (max 330 km / h and autonomy 1,800 km); their replacement was therefore in progress with the SM 79 (maximum speed 425 km / h, and autonomy 2,500 km), planes which despite having provided excellent evidence in Spain were affected by their derivation from a civilian aircraft and which, however, held up comparison with the *Bristol Blenheim* of the British Royal Air Force.
> For hunting there were CR 42s in Libya, similar in performance to the British *Gloster Gladiator*.
> The 50th *Stormo d'assalto* then had Ba.65 for the attack on the ground.
> This is therefore the strength of the approximately three hundred planes located in Libyan airports. As for the Navy, the situation was good in Italy but absolutely insufficient in Libya. The Navy Command of Libya (Admiral Brivonesi) had only a few ships for coastal defense: the cruiser San Giorgio used as a floating battery, four torpedo boats, six gunboats and some submarines.

The Libyan Air Force continued to carry out operations beyond its means. A lack of effective use was also compounded by a quantitative and qualitative lack of available means.
The aircrafts could not be considered adequate under any aspect. The bombers were SM 81 notoriously overtaken for speed (max 330 km / h and autonomy 1,800 km); their replacement was therefore in progress with the SM 79 (maximum speed 425 km / h,

and autonomy 2,500 km), apparatuses which despite having provided excellent evidence in Spain were affected by their derivation from a civilian aircraft and which, however, held up comparison with the Bristol Blenheim of the British Royal Air Force.
As fighters there were in Libya, Fiat CR 42 *Falcos* similar in performance to the British *Gloster Gladiator*.

The 50th *Stormo d'assalto* had *Breda* Ba.65 for the attack on the ground.

This is therefore the strength of the approximately three hundred planes located in Libyan airports. As for the Navy, the situation was adequate in Italy but absolutely insufficient in Libya. The Navy Command of Libya (*Supermarina Libia*, Admiral Brivonesi) had only a few ships for coastal defense: the cruiser *San Giorgio* used as a floating battery, four torpedo boats, six gunboats and some submarines.

On 23 July Graziani sent a report to Badoglio on the military situation in Northern Africa in view of the offensive against Egypt, in which he expressed his concepts and considerations about the situation and which shows what the real Italian military force was. This is a very important document that is worth reporting in full.

Armed Forces' disposition. Land.

The situation that arose following the Italian-French armistice had necessarily given the Cyrenaic chessboard the utmost importance and placed the problem of its defensive strengthening in the foreground.

The 10th Army had come automatically absorbing all the forces and means that had been transferred from Tripolitania to Cyrenaica, while the 5th Army had assumed the character it still retains today as a supply tank. To the 5 divisions initially located in Cyrenaica, two more (the *23 Marzo* and the II Libyan) transferred from Tripolitania had been added, so that in the last decade of June the X Army was made up of three Army Corps. (XXI, XXII, XXIII) with 7 divisions in total. The first operations had then shown that the army's means of fire, and more particularly the mobile artillery, were absolutely insufficient to neutralize the sudden and frequent offenses that the enemy mechanized vehicles operated with impunity on our troops and on our communications, on the back of the defensive border organization, with serious moral consequences.

Hence the determination, implemented even before I reached Tripoli, to transfer from the west to the east most of the mobile artillery of the 5th Army (20mm and 47mm batteries: the entire 20th Artillery Corps Regiment and the 12th Rgt. DF *Savona*).

The effectiveness of this reinforcement of artillery has been fully adequate for a couple of weeks in fact the enemy uses its armored vehicles with much greater caution and without appreciable success.

Arriving in North Africa, I immediately worried about the full defense of the board by examining the possibility that a deprecated collapse of the Tobruck - Porto Bardia system (where the 10th Army is still thickened) could allow the enemy to penetrate theCyrenaic plateau still inhabited by the national and indigenous civil population. I then immediately transferred *Sirte* division to the Barce area (which has already been in place for about ten days), while at the same time I had a flying control system with CC.RR[4] along the foothills: Timimi - El Ezeiat - El Mechil - Zauia - En Neian - El Charruba - Sahabi - Maragh - Augila. Having thus ensured the defense of the region, and in relation to the different offensive task that the Supreme Command had assigned to the forces of North Africa at the end of June, I subsequently created a "Southern Oasis Battlegroup" under the orders of General Maletti, profound connoisseur of the region, with which I

---

[4]*Regi Carabinieri*, Military Police.

aim, as already telegraphed, to operate from Giarabub on Siwa and beyond in the direction of the coast (Marsa Matruth) or the Nile valley, depending on the circumstances.

For a glimpse I will say that this Battlegroup, made up of seven Libyan battalions mostly veterans, light tank units, artillery and three self-loaded Saharian companies, is mostly already collected in Derna and in a dozen days - when will arrive here trucks being shipped from Italy - will also be able to move around its area of use.

In the field of vehicles, similar measures had already made it possible to transfer the majority of efficient trucks located in North Africa with the orders given to me to Cyrenaica (the main reason for my coming to Tripoli) this majority has become almost all. The G.U of Tripolitania keep a number of vehicles strictly necessary for their daily life (to facilitate this I put them all astride the railway): all the rest is or is about to move to Cyrenaica.

At the same time, the automotive workshops - both military and civilian - have intensified the repair of 1800 trucks and the wear and tear, the difficulties and lengths of the routes and the inexperience of the drivers have made them inefficient and the restoration of which will be significantly benefited by the the turnout of specialized personnel requested days ago to the Army General Staff *(tele-avio* 2005 Op of 18 July).

With these provisions and with the competition of civil vehicles, which I squeezed to the last, a very sensitive contribution will be given to the functioning of the automotive service. Lastly, the need to have distribution artillery and adequate counter-battery, when we have to face the semi-field defensive organization of Marsa Matruh, led me to absorb, in favor of the eastern sector, the last 60 100/17mm howitzers and 24 105/28mm guns that were still available in the 5th Army and from today these artillery, all framed in organic units, are marching towards Cyrenaica, where they will constitute a mass of fire under my direct orders. The different constitution that had taken place by assuming the X army as a result of the very first reinforcements, had already suggested to me to give the Armed Forces of Cyrenaica an order better suited to the command and employment possibilities of the G.U. The further conspicuous influx of which I have just mentioned, together with that of the IV tanker infantry of Italy, has made a new order mandatory.

This is now in force and is summarized in the attached mirror.

To clarify it, I add that I wanted to place General Gallina in the "Libyan Divisions Group" because the different training direction given to the two divisions and the moral consequences suffered in particular by the Ist Libyan Division (following the painful episodes of the period 11-16 June) made it urgent to give a vigorous moral and material impulse to the two units for their further use on the battlefield. In this way, the commander of the tenth army, with which all or part of the Libyan divisions group may be decentralized, will also be able to make use of the experienced ability of General Gallina.

This different grouping of forces is naturally reflected in the organization of the Intendenza, which, while continuing to depend on the Superior Command, will constitute its own delegation to the X Army and will directly provide for the needs of the other G.U. It is also reflected in the organization of the CC.RR, whose territorial and mobile service is now headed solely by the Higher Command of the Army, to which I have also entrusted the task of coastal surveillance of the Militia, whose components, almost all farmers, I have demobilized because they are more profitably awaiting the urgent work of the campaign.

Always in this order of ideas, since the recall of the members of the ordinary Militia had put in crisis not only the agricultural work, but also all the other activities and vital needs of the colony, I arranged that the four MVSN battalions already existing in Africa Northern (all four in precarious conditions of strength, armament and training) are contracted in a single training department, selecting the components and equipping it with adequate armament. This department will soon be able to take its place among the Army's operating units.

Operative Directives.

I have already outlined my broad operational concepts. More details I will give at the opportune moment of the development that the operations will be able to assume, both for the strictly terrestrial part and for what it has drawn to the defense from the presumable offenses that can be directed against us by enemy naval forces during our advance. Pending the completion of the deployment of forces and above all of the means (subordinated to the arrival of the well-known convoy from Italy), the 10th Army is fully attested at the border with its five organic divisions.
Within reach are the two Libyan divisions. The two fortresses of Tobruk and Porto Bardia [are] in full efficiency.
The communications between them controlled by us.
Giarabub Oasis [is] adequately guarded, albeit under wide-ranging control of enemy mobile forces.
The orders given to the 10th Army must guarantee us the firm possession of the Forte Capuzzo, to which the enemy aims tenaciously in the dual purpose of removing our future offensive starting base and completing the occupation system it carried out in the first days of operations. along the border track Porto Bardia - Giarabub (road junctions and wells of Sidi– Omar - Bir– Esch– Sceferzen –Scegga - Uescechet - Ed Heira), occupations which it advantageously exploits as the collection and departure bases of its mechanized units and for block all traffic with Giarabub. In this regard, I add that I have already budgeted the re-employment - at the time - of these nodes that may be of interest to us for offensive operations and that the garrison of Giarabub, hitherto provided by means of refueling launched from the plane, can now take advantage of the plane - transport - as he was able to restore the landing field.
The activity of our departments - generally self-loaded - along the frontier belt is constant. As I said earlier, this activity has paralyzed the troublesome dripping of British armored cars. Essentially contributed to this was the assignment to our mobile columns of large artillery rates of 20, 47 and 65/17mm self-ptopelled, whose immediate and well coordinated use has proven to be very effective.

Use of air force.

The problem of anti-aircraft defense is affected, among all the war organizations, by the major deficiencies.
The same is true of the naval defense of harbours. The defense of Tripoli, Benghazi, Derna and even Tobruk and Porto Bardia - so frequently exposed to enemy air and naval incursions and offenses - does not serve the purpose at all.
Suffice it to mention that Benghazi has four 75/27mm batteries on wheeled carriages, occasionally posted on parapets; Derna of a few machine guns and Tripoli itself of an equipment and organization totally unequal to the needs.
This consideration and the fact that Tripoli's landing is not immune to offense, led me to discard a transfer of vehicles from Tripoli to Benghazi. I limited myself to disarming Zuara of the four 77/28mm batteries available to arm Benghazi but with all this I believe that the damage of a bombing of Benghazi in the particular conditions of activity in which the port is working today and the presence of conspicuous military objectives etc. they would be of incalculable gravity. Knowing the difficulties that exist in the Motherland on the subject, I did not want to make particular requests.
  I can only conclude that the problem exists in all its seriousness and urgency and that

any provision that could be implemented on the matter would be of vital utility. Various Provisions

In parallel with the provisions mentioned above, other provisions have been implemented or are being implemented.
I mention only those that acquire greater importance, for the purposes of the beneficial efficiency of North Africa. that is, they require the disposition of the central authority.
The convoy system offers the greatest guarantees; but of course it is not the fastest.
This is confirmed by the delay with which the train currently under construction in Italy is currently being implemented.
It does not seem to me to be discarded the aid of medium or small tonnage steamers which, reaching Tripoli along the Tunisian-Tripoline coast and therefore without any escort, can constitute a continuous, albeit not substantial, contribution to the problem of supplies. This system is currently being followed between Tripolitania and Cyrenaica and particularly from Benghazi to Derna, Tobruk and Porto Bardia with satisfactory results.

Harbours' utilization.

The Benghazi service has been unified with the establishment of a single similar Provisional Commissioner for Tobruk. *Supermarina* allowed the establishment of a passing base in Ain Gazala, to serve only as a depot for fuel. In addition to G.a F.[5], six Divisions of the 5th army are currently in Tripolitania (about 60,000 men).
This, necessarily, dismembered of its artillery and impoverished of vehicles, has lost all vitality. The weight of feeding such a large contingent therefore remains, whereas for military purposes it could be reduced to a couple of divisions, repatriating the remaining forces. However, this is a decision involving political and security problems, for the purpose of returning to the homeland, by sea, of many tens of thousands of men. As such, it is beyond my competence; I also considered mentioning it both for moral reasons and for the immediate and mediated logistical benefit that would result.
A similar problem is urgent for the thousands of skilled workers in the defensive works of western Libya, whose continuation is naturally bound to the political-military situations that will come about on that frontier. I hope to solve this problem myself, when it is sure that diverting these workers from the current activity does not result in unemployment for them, or in an absorption of trucks so jealously recovered or, when you want to transfer them to Cyrenaica, for road works or other, in an aggravation of logistics. The best solution, however, would be to allocate the rate of them that cannot be further used as soon as possible.

In Egypt General Archibald Wavell was able to dispose of about 36,000 including Indian and New Zealand units, while in Palestine there were another 27,500 men. In practice, the frontline troops of the *Western Desert Force* (formed June 17, 1940) consisted of an Armored Division with two tank regiments for each brigade, and a British infantry brigade. All units had insufficient armament and transport and artillery equipment; the 7th *Armored Division* had 65 MK VI cruiser tanks out of the 220 planned.

Western Desert Force:

Commander-in-Chief, Middle East: General Sir Archibald Wavell
Commander *Western Desert Force*: Lieutenant-General R. N. O'Connor;

---

[5]*Guardia alla Frontiera*, Border Guards.

Corps Troops:

7th Battalion, *Royal Tank Regiment* (*Matilda* tanks)
1st *Royal Horse Artillery*
104th *Royal Horse Artillery*
51st *Field Regiment* R.A.
7th *Medium Regiments* R.A.
64th *Medium Regiments* R.A.

7th *Armoured Division*:

4th *Armoured Brigade*
7th *Armoured Brigade*
Support Group (Infantry Brigade)
divisional troops

4th *Indian Division*:

5th *Indian Infantry Brigade*
11th *Indian Infantry Brigade*
divisional troops
i
16th *Infantry Brigade* (with the 4th *Indian Division*).

The typical British infantry division of the day consisted of three brigades of three battalions each, a machine gun battalion and three regiments of artillery, usually each of twenty-four 25-pounder field guns. Also attached would be a regiment of 2-pounder AT guns. A British infantry division would usually have about 13,600 men, while the Australian and New Zealand divisions would be about 20-25% stronger. The first corps was formed in January of 1941 (the XIII), while the first army was created on 24 September of 1941 (the 8th). A British armored division had 9,600 men. So, it is always good to recall that a Commonwealth division would be larger and would have a great deal more artillery and AT weapons than an Italian division. They would often have a divisional cavalry unit assigned, which would be a partly motorized and mechanized battalion, sometimes including light tanks, which the Italian infantry division lacked until later in the war.
Early on, the British began organizing a tactical unit called the *"jock column."* This was named for Lieutenant Colonellater Major General"Jock" Campbell who died after Operation *Crusader* in an auto mishap. These jock columns were small formation columns made up of infantry, armor and artillery, similar to the Italian *Gruppi* but were too weak for the most part to be compared with the German *Kampfgruppe* . Jock himselfsaid that a jock column could do any thing with two exceptions. *They could not capture ground from the enemy or deny ground to the enemy."* He also stated on another occasion that, *as soon as we get the enemy where we want him, we must drop dispersed columns and*

concentrate every available gun. These controversial columns were used from the summer of 1940 until 1942

The British navy, with her Allies, would suffer losses throughout the war and never halt Italy's effort to supply Libya. But the Royal Navy did affect the land war in many direct ways, especially in the early part of the war. Through naval gunfire support from battleships, cruisers, and destroyers, to naval resupply operations to Tobruk, the White Ensign made a positive contribution to the Allied cause. With the arrival of the Luftwaffe with its deadly anti-shipping capability, and later with naval strength being siphoned off to fight Japan, the Allied navies had less of a direct impact on the war. Yet a new role developed which would always be there for the rest of the war the possibility of an amphibious landing in the Axis rear. The Axis would constantly have troops, usually at divisional strength, deployed in the rear to combat this threat. This card was only played once, in the abortive raid on Tobruk on 13/14 September 1942.

The Commonwealth situation in the air was shaky, but the British did have the effective Hurricane fighter in the Middle East, and a trans-Africa air route (the so called "*Takoradi air route*") was inaugurated early to allow for shipment of airplanes across Africa and down the Nile to Egypt, thus eliminating the need to ship these planes by sea. The Commonwealth air units fared well not only against the Italian air force, but against the best of the *Luftwaffe*, the superior Me-109 fighter[6].

As of 1939, a plan was in concrete implementation phase which as basic data included six Divisions in Egypt (with three regiments) and three Divisions in Palestine (transportable to Egypt in case of need).

By early June 1940 British forces in Egypt were practically ready. The Italian Military Information System was aware of the true extent of these forces.

In all, the forces "present in Egypt in early June 1940 were estimated at around 100,000–105,000 men: 40,000 British, 15,000 Indians, 7,000 New Zealanders, 1,500 Rhodesians and 40,000 Egyptians.

They were career troops, equipped with excellent training, wide suitability of vehicles to maneuver off-road at considerable speed, perfect organization of land and aircraft connections, availability of armored cars and tanks particularly suitable for war in the desert, intrinsic superiority of tanks in armament, speed and maneuverability and the efficiency of a modern artillery, motorized and superior for caliber and range. To these positive factors were added the negative Italian ones: the poor training of cadres and troops, the availability of vehicles limited to the point of imposing a choice between transport of units or supplies, the multiple types of vehicles mostly unsuitable for moving off-road, the light three-ton tanks with more deficiencies than good qualities, the artillery largely outdated, the embryonic anti-tank defense and the non-existent or almost non-existent anti-aircraft defense.

The spearheads in the British Army were formed by the 7th Armored Division and the Indian 4th Indian Division.

The British army was primarily concerned about water shortages and the complexities of motorization; the navy feared for the safety of the floating dry docks on which the operational possibilities of the fleet depended. In essence, the main problem was only one, the underlying one for any operational plan: the logistical problem. But the psychological attitude was different from that of the Italian leaders: Wavell believed that

---

[6] Green, Massignani 1994, p.25

the Italian numerical advantage was significantly reduced by a slightly aggressive morale and some significant limitations in the field of materials.

On August 16, 1940 Churchill compiled the General Directives for the supreme commander in the Middle East. These directives were as follows:

1) The large-scale invasion of Egypt by Libya must now be expected at all times. It is therefore necessary to gather and distribute the greatest possible forces along and towards the western border. Any political and administrative considerations must be duly subordinated to this need.

2) The available forces are as follows: the British armored forces in Egypt, the four British battalions of Marsa Matruh, the two of Alexandria and the two of Cairo, total 8 battalions; the three battalions of the Canale area; the British reserve brigade from Palestine, ie 14 infantry battalions of regular troops; the New Zealand brigade, the Australian brigade of Palestine; the Polish brigade; part of the Union Brigade from East Africa; the 4th Indian division now behind Marsa Matruh; the new Indian division; the 11,500 men arriving in Suez, all the artillery (150 guns) now in the Middle East or traveling from India; the Egyptian army in everything in which it can be used as an active service.

3) Tactical use of the aforesaid force. Marsa Matruh's position must be fully fortified as soon as possible. The sector held by three Egyptian battalions must be taken over by the three British battalions, so as to make that force homogeneous. This will have to be done even if the Egyptian government wants to withdraw the artillery now in the hands of these three battalions. The possibility of supplying the position of Marsa Matruh by sea troops and of cutting enemy communications, when the Italians have passed over, heading for the Delta, must be studied with the supreme commander of the Mediterranean Fleet. Otherwise you may prefer a descent on the communications of Sollum and even further west.

All water supplies between the defenses of Marsa Matruh and Alexandria must be depotable. No attempt should be made to leave squads to defend the wells near the coast in this region. The Indian 4th division will have to withdraw to Alexandria when necessary, or be evacuated by sea. The road from Sollum to Marsa Matruh and even more the paved road from Marsa Matruh to Alexandria must be made intransitable, when abandoned, by delayed-burst mines or by chemical treatment of the asphalt surface.

4) In this way the Nile Army will await the Italian invasion. It is to be expected that the enemy will advance with great forces, slowing down only, but bitterly, by the scarcity of water and fuel. It will certainly have considerable armored forces to contain and repel our poorest, unless these are improved in time by the armored regiment from Great Britain. If he cannot destroy it, he will cover Marsa Matruh. But if the main line of the Delta, diligently fortified and firmly held, the enemy will be forced to field an army whose supplies of water, oil, food and ammunition will be very difficult.

When this army was seriously engaged, the action against its lines of communication from Marsa Matruh, by bombing the sea, attacking Sollum, or even much further west, would be a fatal blow to it.

OPERAZIONE E:
THE ITALIAN ADVANCE ON SIDI EL BARRANI.

On July 15 Badoglio ordered that the 10th Army be ready to move; immediately afterwards Badoglio himself asked for a postponement - for climatic reasons - of the action at the end of October. Graziani agreed, but just a month later, on August 15, Mussolini himself telegraphed that the invasion of England was decided (in a week or a month) and that he would have to attack concurrently, adding to take - in this regard - any responsibility.

Graziani, for his part, had ordered to organize, just for that date, a fast armored column - corresponding roughly to a training brigade, but immediately after, on the 19th, he suspended the implementation of what he himself ordered on 13, with an urgent encrypted telegram addressed to the 10th Army, motivating the counterorder with the fact that the planned column would have been excessively heavy and would have removed many means of fire from the army.

On day 15, it was decided to reunite the existing tanks (L 3 and M 11/39) in a Tank Command of Libya, under the orders of General Valentino Babini, articulated on:

- 1st *Raggruppamento Carri* (col. Aresca), with a btl. of M tanks and 3 btll L tanks; intended to operate with the 23rd Army Corps;

- 2nd *Raggruppamento Carri* (col. Trivioli), with one btl M tanks (on one cp.) and 3 btll. L tanks, intended to operate with the Libyan Divisions group;

- 1 btg. mixed tanks (1 cp. M tanks and 1 cp. L tanks) intended to operate with the Maletti Group;

- LX btg. L tanks (minus one company) intended to operate with the XXIst Corps.

With this formation, the *Raggruppamento Carri*Aresca took part in the advance in Egypt.

The chronic lack of vehicles meant that only the XXIIIrd Army Corps, led by Annibale Bergonzoli, the Libyan Divisions Group and the Libyan motorized grouping (otherwise known as the *Raggruppamento Maletti*), would participate in the offensive towards Egypt only forces with vehicles. The XXIII had about a thousand means of transport that went to truck the 1st Black Shirts Division *23 Marzo*, while the *Marmarica* and *Cirene* Divisions would have moved on foot. The Libyan Divisions Group had approximately 650 means of transport which were intended for the transport of artillery, light tanks, water, food, ammunition and fuel for three days of autonomy. The Maletti Group had about 450 vehicles and was not only fully truck-mounted but also capable of considerable logistical autonomy (about 700 km).

The remaining Army Corps, XXI and XXII, were instead deployed as reserves. The XXI sided in the Cyrene area and the XXII in defense of the Tobruk base.

Fort (*Ridotta*) Capuzzo on the Libyan- Egyptian border
(Kurt Caesar,1941.Author's collection)

A first offensive plan was assessed in the days between 22 and 25 August 1940. It was a limited offensive aimed at securing the Cyrenaean border.

The advance would take place over three columns. the first would have advanced from Capuzzo towards Sollum; the second towards Gabr Bu Tares, the third, following the southernmost route, towards Sceferzer and Bir El Chreigat. This plan aimed to bring Italian troops to the edge of Hagiag el Aqasa but considered too modest as an ambition was shelved. A second floor was therefore studied and presented on September 3, 1940. It included a column, composed of the XXIII Army Corps., Advanced from Capuzzo towards Sollum and then Sidi El Barrani. A southernmost column, with the Libyan Divisions Group and the Maletti Group, was to advance along the Sceferzer-Der el Brugg-Der el Hamr-Bir Habata-Bir er Rabia-Bir Enba route. This plan should have been followed by the Italians. Graziani was primarily concerned about the southern column. There would have been difficulties connecting between the two columns due to the edge of Hagiag El Aqasa.

Graziani then predicted a disconnect between the Maletti grouping and the Libyan Divisions as the infantry of the latter would move on foot; Graziani also believed that the Maletti Group would be too weak to face the British forces. This produced a further change that was made close to the offensive.

All forces would have advanced on a single line, the coastal one. The offensive plan envisaged that the Libyan Divisions would open the door while the *Marmarica* and Cirene Divisions remained in the second row.

The Black Shirts Division *23 Marzo* and the 1st *Raggruppamento Carri* were placed in reserve. The Maletti group had the task of guaranteeing the right flank of the deployment from possible incursions from the south.

At dawn on September 13, 1940, the cross-border advance on Sollum and Halfaya, whose codename was Operation E, began; in the evening at 20 the situation was as follows:

the 1st Libyan Division had occupied Sollum;

the 2nd Libyan Division had occupied Passo Halfaya;

the *Cirene* Division was behind the 2nd Libyan Div.

the Maletti Group from Sidi Omar, along the border, had reached Neguet Ghirba (N.O. of Sidi Omar)

the *Marmarica* Division from Bir Hafid had entered Egypt reaching Gabr bu Amud;

the Black Shirt Division *23 Marzo* from Gabr el Ahmar had reached the border in Gabr Asceran.

At 8 pm on September 14, while the two Libyan Divisions had advanced on the plain, between the sea and the ridge, for about 20 km. beyond Sollum, *Cirene* was on the ridge south of Halfaya, the *23 Marzo* had crossed the border and had reached the Musaid area, between Capuzzo and Sollum; the Maletti Group was located west of Sidi Omar. The enemy retreated offering sporadic resistance from armored units.

On September 15, a motorized column was organized at the Command of General Bergonzoli, constituted by the *23 Marzo*. and the Maletti Group with rates of troops of C.A. The column, bypassing the Libyan Divisions, aimed at Sidi el Barrani. The *23 Marzo* Division was divided into two blocks: on the right the 233rd Black Shirts Legion under the command of Console Generale Nìccolo Nicchiarelli (Cons. Gen. Olivas), with a grouping of light tanks, on the left the 219th Legion, with divisional artillery.

The climb, carried out amidst many difficulties due to the bad tracks on which 450 vehicles passed, was completed only at 11.30 am, heavily disturbed by the enemy artillery and mechanized vehicles. Furthermore, the streets had been mined and the wells salty; coastal artery devastated.

On the evening of September 15 the troops were east of Buq Buq and the Division *23 Marzo* already at 25 km. by Sidi el Barrani. Once the advance was resumed at the first light of the 16th, the left column (219th Legion) was soon engaged. A precise, rapid, centered artillery fire slowed down its movement several times, forcing it to proceed on foot for some stretches. On foot they move the CXIV Battailon to the left and the CXVIII Battailon to the right. An angry and quick shot is unleashed on them. The Black Shirts advanced the same by bending a little towards the sea. The Italian artillery countered the opposing one and the forward movement was resumed and accelerated, arousing the admiration of Gen. Bergonzoli. At around 1pm, with slow movement due to the sandy soil and a detour to the south to escape the enemy shot, the right column came very close to the town, making its threat felt. The enemy was forced to quickly fold up its artillery and the left column could certainly continue on the target without other difficulties. At 14.15 the column on the right, which had already made contact with its tankers launched to attack enemy vehicles, reached the coast at 4-5 km east of Sidi el Barrani. At the same time the commander of the *23 Marzo* Division entered Sidi el Barrani at the head of the 219th Black Shirts Legion . On the evening of the same day 16 the location of Graziani's troops was as follows:

1st Black Shirts Division *23 Marzo* - 10 km. east of Sidi el Barrani, from the sea to Samet-Omm - Himeisa.
Maletti Group - 5 km. east of the town.
I Libyan Division - 15 Km. West of Sidi el Barrani, straddling the coast road.
2 Libyan Division - on the southern slope, in Sawani el Khur.
Cirene Division in Bir Siuyat (south east of Halfaya).
Marmarica Division in Gat bu Fares (south of Capuzzo).

The total losses of Italian troops in the operational period from 13 to 18 September are divided as follows:

23 Marzo Division: 187.
Marmarica Division: 12.
Army Corps troops: 140.
Cirene Division: 16.
Maletti Group: 69.

The outcome of the operation was favorable to the Italians. The troops showed high warrior qualities and loyalty to duty despite the exceptional adverse conditions of terrain, climate and ghibli storms. Our soldiers, forced to rest on the bare ground, harassed by mice, scorpions and chameleons, resisting the high temperatures and the strong changes of these, fed with salmon and canned meat, tormented by thirst, beautifully faced the crisis of supplies ; they dug ditches in the sand dunes to collect the water that the overheated atmosphere of the day gave to the ground cooling off during the night. The inefficiency and consequent uselessness of the L light tanks was immediately demonstrated

Regardless of the weak armor and poor armament, of the 52 employed in the advance, at the end of the operation only 17 light tanks were efficient.

The report on the operations for the capture of Sidi Barrani summarized the action of the Aresca' tanks as follows:

[...]
7th - Aresca Group - The tanks, both M and L, all tracked the motorized column. These were two difficult days for the tanks, especially as the "*ghibli*" complicated the environment by making the temperature of the tanks exceed from 10 to 16 (they reached 70 °). Towards the end of the 2 operating days there were several faintings of pilots.

- The average speed maintained by the motorized column was too high for tracked wagons. They kept constantly striving and failures followed, which were inevitable under such conditions. On the other hand, it was not possible to regulate the gear differently, in order not to produce separations in the column that could have created serious difficulties in the event of meeting the enemy. It is therefore appropriate that the "motorized column" regulates the gear on the less rapid vehicle, which it cannot do without for its safety.

- An unitary use of the M and L tanks was lacking, in the culminating phase of the action on Sidi Barrani also due to the nature of the bottom of the land which made it almost impossible, due to excessive failures, to profitably use the L wagons (situation of wagons predicted at term action 17 efficient out of 52).

There is no doubt, however, that an armored unit of the type of the grouping in question cannot fail, in this environment and against an enemy equipped with strong armored elements, to give a decisive contribution in the decisive phase of the action with an action to wide range, if the characteristics of light wagons have improved.

The operations that led to the capture of Sidi el Barrani were summarized in the War Bulletins issued by the Supreme Command, not always responding to reality:

BULLETIN N ° 100 - September 15
In Cyrenaica our advanced departments have crossed the border and engaged in lively fights against opposing elements. Our air force actively participates, attacking with bombing and grazing flights concentrations of enemy mechanized vehicles. Two Blenheim-type opposing aircraft have been shot down.

BULLETIN No. 101 - September 16
Our vanguards have occupied and passed Sollum. About fifty enemy tanks and armored cars were destroyed. Retreating enemy departments have set fire to numerous deposits and suffered severe losses from the very intense action of our air force.

BULLETIN N ° 102 - September 17
Yesterday, fierce fighting took place in the Sidi el Barrani region between our advancing troops and English armored formations. In the midst of clouds of sand raised by the fiery Sahara ghibli, the battle continues. You notice some symptoms of crisis in the enemy deployment.

BULLETIN No. 103 - September 18
In northern Africa, metropolitan troops and Libyan troops - which also in this action have fully confirmed their high warlike virtues and absolute loyalty to Italy - continuing in their victorious advance they occupied Sidi el Barrani, 100 km in line of air from the old Cyrenaic border, and they are proceeding with the organization of the new base and rear areas. The tenacious resistance of the enemy - supported by armored formations - has been shattered everywhere. Our air force has repeatedly intervened with bombing and strafing actions. Five enemy Gloster-type appliances fell into flames, one was probably shot down. Four of our planes have not returned to the base.

As for the reactions in Rome to the evolution of African events, Galeazzo Ciano noted in his Diary about the developments of *Operation E* and the state of mind of the *Duce*, at first skeptical towards Marshal Graziani, whose replacement he promoted, and so on increasingly euphoric way:

September 7, 1940. Council of Ministers. At the end of the session, the Duce makes some political statements. He begins by stating that in his opinion the war is now destined to last beyond winter, although he certainly believes that the Germans will land in England. As far as we are directly concerned, he has redone the history of the attack on Egypt: it should have started today, except that Graziani has asked for an extension of one month. Badoglio was in favor of the extension. Mussolini denied it, taking responsibility for the decision upon himself. If Graziani does not attack on Monday, he will be replaced. And also to the navy he gave the order to move towards the British fleet and fight. For the more distant future, he said that he is now sure that between 1945 and 1950 the war will break out between the Axis and Russia. By that time he would have already set up the armaments program, based on one hundred Divisions.

September 8, 1940. Graziani replied that he obeys: the attack will begin tomorrow. Many military technicians are skeptical. Among others, the Prince of Piedmont who made the largest reservations with me on the possibility and opportunity of the company. The naval clash has not yet taken place, especially since the aerial reconnaissance has not identified the route of the Gibraltar team.

September 9, 1940. The attack on Egypt suffered a new delay. Graziani is closing down and preparing to begin the action on the 12. Never has a military operation been carried out so reluctantly by the commanders.

September 11, 1940. The start of the attack on Egypt is confirmed for tomorrow. Even General Carboni, who has never made optimism cheap, says that the arrival in Marsa Matruh is easy and in Alessandria possible.

September 13, 1940. Ribbentrop calls from Berlin: he wants to come to Rome next week to confer on two topics: Russia and America. The idea of travel can be useful. I give the approval. Graziani should have attacked, but so far we have no precise information.

September 14, 1940. The attack on Egypt has begun. The British, for now, are withdrawing without fighting. They want to move us away from the bases and lengthen our supply routes. The Duce, who has recovered in a good mood, considers the arrival in

Marsa Matruh as a great victory, above all because then our air force will be able to attack Alexandria escorted by hunting, that is, by day.

September 16, 1940. Mussolini is excited about the trend for the march in Egypt. But he is angry with Berti, who for his slowness would have made us lose the spoils. The fact is that no fighting has taken place so far: only a few rearguard battles.

September 17, 1940. Things in Egypt seem to be getting better and better. The British retreat with unexpected speed. According to military experts, resistance will take place in Marsa Matruh: others believe instead in Alexandria. Mussolini is radiant: he has taken the entire responsibility for the offensive on his shoulders and is proud to have been right.

For the summary of the operations carried out from September 14 to September 17, it is very important to read the Historical Diary of the Supreme Command, a document as fundamental as it is little known:

September 14, 1940.
Operations in Egypt.
Marshal Graziani informs: The situation at 18.00 on the 13th was the following:
- First Libyan Division: Neqb el Asida
- Second Libyan Division: Halfaia Pass
- XXIII C.A in second row
- Maletti Group: Ghirba
- During the day of the 13th, the advance was strongly opposed by armored vehicles and enemy aviation.
-Morning of September 14, the advance was resumed.

September 15, 1940.
Operations in Egypt.
Marshal Graziani informs: the advance of our columns continued throughout the day of the 14th.
Situation at 6 pm on September 14th:
- First Libyan Division: Bir Thidan el Khadim (25 km from Bug Bug);
- Second Libyan Division: on the right is almost the height of the First D.L.
- Maletti column moving on Halfaia;
- *Cirene* Division: in Bir Siuyat.
The advance was strongly opposed by enemy armoured vehicles supported by artillery and aviation. To date, a dozen tanks and armored cars and thirty vehicles have been destroyed in combat.
This morning the decisive maneuver of swift elements began on Sidi-el-Barrani.
As regards the air activity, Marshal Graziani communicates:
- During the day of the 14th, in relation to the land operations in progress, intense air activity was carried out;
- During the night our planes repeatedly bombed airports and plants in El Dab'à, causing large fires;
- Our bombing and grazing flight formations have subjected to effective offenses, concentrations of mechanized enemies between Bir el Chreigat and Der el Brugh and Bir Hamra;

- In combat with enemy planes, which have bombed our troops (minor damages), two fighters were shot down.

September 16, 1940.
The situation of the Italian forces on the evening of September 15 was the following:
- Division *XXIII Marzo*: 10 km east of Bug Bug;
- Libyan Divisions Group: between Bug Bug and El Sauani el Hilwa;
- Maletti Group: 15 km from Bug Bug;
- The enemy withdrew all the vehicles from Bir El Chreigat to Bir Sofafi (south route) setting fire to all the deposits and suffering serious losses due to our intense air action (12 assault aircraft and 12 fighter aircraft carried out two actions of fragmentation and strafing of motorized vehicles in retreat).
- A total of 82 CR.42 devices took turns in protecting our running columns.
At dawn on 16 September the advance on Sidi – el – Barrani was resumed.
At about 15.30, the troops of the *23 Marzo* Division occupied this location by winning the tenacious resistance still opposed by the 64th English Armored Division.
Our motorized units chase the enemy towards Marsa Matruh and south towards Bir Enba, Bir Rabia, Bir Sofafi, to cut the retreat into strong mechanized enemy nuclei that result in that area.

September 17, 1940.
The High Commander A.S.I[7] communicates:
- No results of the chase actions carried out by our units towards Marsa Matruh and south, in the direction of Bir Enba, Bir er Rabia, Bir Sofafi, to cut the retreat to strong enemy motorized nuclei, which yesterday 16 were still in those areas;
- Reservation to communicate further information on the situation which is currently being settled.
Marshal Graziani:
- Points out that, from the imposing genius problems are taking, it is essential to send a general of the weapon, whose name he indicates;
- Represents that after the occupation of Sidi-el-Barrani a long stop becomes indispensable:
- To concentrate other means;
- For the needs of rearranging the units after 8 days of movement in almost prohibitive climatic conditions;
- To allow the flow of supplies to an area devoid of all resources, including water, since the British made the numerous wells existing in Sidi el Barrani unusable;
- Due to the absolute necessity of arranging the road from Sollum to Sidi-el-Barrani, (the existing track is almost impractical).

September 18, 1940.
Marshal Graziani communicates:
- Our troops are consolidating the occupation of Sidi el Barrani, extending it towards south-east;
- The night on the 18th, was characterized by intense enemy air-naval activity (bombing of Sidi el Barrani and from the coast between Sollum and Bardia, and by repeated aerial actions against Sidi el Barrani) countered by the effective reaction of our aviation.

---

[7]A.S.I. *Africa Settentrionale Italiana*, Italian North Africa.

The losses suffered by the Italians throughout the period from 13 to 18 September amounted to 120 dead and 410 wounded, a third of which were Libyan *ascari*.

Many vehicles were damaged more by the wear and tear suffered in that desert environment than by the effect of the enemy offense.

The 5a *Squadra Aerea* lost six aircraft, two of them from various accidents. The British casualties reported by Wavell were less than 50 men with a modest number of damaged or captured vehicles.

In his *Report* sent to the Supreme Command on September 18, Graziani concluded triofally:

> One wonders when the British will begin to understand that they are dealing with the strongest colonial army in the world and when they will finally learn about the value of the Italian soldier. They will learn it as soon as possible.

On September 29 Graziani reached Rome and met the *Duce* in his office in Palazzo Venezia, after Badoglio had summoned him to Italy on the orders of Mussolini. After questioning Graziani about the general situation of the offensive just completed in Egypt, the *Duce* ordered to reach Marsa Matruh in October. Mussolini ended the interview with the following words

> The month of July gave us English Somalia, September Sidi el Barrani, October will be able to give us Marsa Matruh. This will allow us to carry on our air force which will then be able to push the bombing on Alexandria. In itself, Marsa Matruh is but a name, but what matters is that we proceed forward. On the other hand, I never fixate on territorial objectives. As a result of these directives, you will be able to resume the march in mid-October.

Graziani replied that he had to return to Libya before giving a judgment on the feasibility of the advance, but made reservations for a subsequent rush to Marsa Matruh.

As soon as he left Palazzo Venezia, Graziani went to talk to the Foreign Minister, Count Galeazzo Ciano, son-in-law of Mussolini. In Graziani's defensive memorial there is an excerpt from his personal diary. On the date of September 30 (page 101 of the memorial) there is the summary of Marescillo's conversation with Ciano.

> This morning I was received by Count Ciano who welcomes me with great cordiality. He argues about the resumption of operations in Libya and asks me about it.
>
> I clearly explain to him what had happened today and I specify that I do not see the possibility of moving towards October 15th at all.
>
> Conte Ciano then tells me that this urgency is imposed by political reasons and adds that the Duce has great confidence in me and that he sees with pleasure the possibility that I, in this war, as a national leader, may rise to the international one.
>
> I reply that I am very flattered by the Duce's benevolence and esteem, but that, precisely because I feel proud of it, I cannot let myself be carried away by ambitions that could lead me to very bitter consequences and which I believe with this to serve in true loyalty and honesty of intent the homeland and the Duce himself.
>
> Count Ciano tries to insist to convince me, but I confirm my point of view, that is that, before moving forward, it is necessary to give life to the necessary organization, and to

the influx of the missing means - which may occur in mid-December .

Ciano then tells me: What if the Duce gives you the order to move?

In this case I answer, there are two cases; or I refuse and then I can also incur the penal code - or I blindly obey and then you can face a defeat of which I will not be responsible.

I conclude by asking him to represent to the *Duce* that however, for my part, nothing will be neglected to speed up the time and we agree that if I have to send documents of serious interest to the General Staff, I will simultaneously send a copy to him who will return it to the *Duce* in secret. Thus ends the interview.

In Count Ciano's *Diary*, on the date of October 2, 1940 we read, regarding the conversation with Graziani:

The Duce is very much launched for an upcoming attack on Marsa Matruh and is irritated with Badoglio because he has ruled out that the action can be carried out in October. I speak about it with Graziani, because the Duce wants to know how he actually thinks. Graziani believes he has to wait a long time - at least throughout November - to complete the logistical preparation, the only, true, definitive guarantee of success. He fears that the British will hold out in Marsa Matruh for a long enough period: if our supplies do not work, it would be necessary to withdraw. E. in the desert, the retreat is a route.

These considerations, reported by Ciano to Mussolini, did not concern the *Duce* who, on the contrary, had met on the Brenner with Hitler on October 4, during which summits the Führer had offered German aid, which the Duce refused. Ciano wrote:

The *Duce* then lays out his war plan regarding Egypt. He says that shortly we will move on to the second phase of the offensive that will bring our troops to Marsa Matruh and expounds the strategic importance of this objective. Finally, the third phase of the offensive that will take us on the Nile Delta and the occupation of Alexandria will take place. The *Führer*, pointing out that the Italians are participating with the air forces in the fight against the British Isles, offers the Duce the contribution of his specialized forces for the attack on Egypt. The *Duce* answers by thanking and saying that he does not need any help for the second phase of the offensive, while he reserves the right to let the Führer know how useful he could be for the third phase. As of now, however, he can say that the only things that could be needed are trucks, a rate of heavy wagons and some formations of *Stukas*.

The *Führer* declares that he is ready to provide such means when he makes known the most opportune moment has come.

Mussolini had therefore gone to the Rocca delle Caminate, his castle near Forlì, from where he had drawn up a note for Badoglio to be delivered to Graziani before his return to Libyan territory.

Mussolini gave directives for the development of operations in Egypt:

1. The taking of Sidi el Barrani was an indisputable brilliant tactical success and an equally indisputable political success as it brought about a crisis in the Egyptian government and revealed a division in the political class of that country.

2. Only with the taking of Marsa Matruh will tactical success become strategic and may have even more important consequences from a political point of view.

3. The operation on Marsa Matruh must begin by 10/15 of this month since it is my belief that the means currently available to Graziani are sufficient for the purpose and in the set time. The staff are almost intact. Clear superiority - at present - of artillery, tanks, airplanes.

Superiority in morale. All this results from Graziani's very interesting oral report.

The logistical problem remains, which has only one particularly serious aspect: that of water. But less water is needed in October than in the height of summer.

4. The caterpillar and other Graziani requests can be met as far as possible and will always arrive in good time if it is for the moment when we have to engage the great battle on the Delta.

5. The desert temperature of October is tolerable for Italian troops that are now loose, but it can always be hard for people from the north or new people who have not yet trained.

6. It is my belief that the British will not defend Marsa Matruh except to the extent strictly necessary to delay our march and disengage their formations.

7. It is true that postponing the attack in November, other material is sent to Cyrenaica, but it is equally true that the British are strengthened in equal and perhaps greater measure. It is now proven that the attacker cannot waste time.

8. The Sicilian Channel must be sealed so that nothing more from the west arrives, since the activity of our aviation in the A.O., for known reasons, can only moderately disturb the convoys passing through the Red Sea.

9. Once in Marsa Matruh, we will see which of the two pillars of the English Mediterranean defense should be demolished: whether Egypt or the Greece.

It was Greece. Visconti Prasca's Italian troops crossed the Epirot border on the night of October 28, in what was to be a military walk on the Greek sun, that soon turned into a nightmare in mud, rain and snow.

The day after the invasion of Greece, the 29th, Graziani was again invited to attack Marsa Matruh. Mussolini wrote to him that

… It makes no sense to have 16 months to prepare, have 15 divisions available and just take Sidi el-Barrani home.

In early November 1940 the III *Carri M* Battalion arrived in Libya with the first 37 M13-40 medium tanks. In the meantime, the Libyan Tank Command was transformed into a Special Armored Brigade, commanded by General Babini on 25 November; General Berti for health reasons temporarily left the command of the 10th Army to General Gariboldi who assumed the interim command.

Soon the Greek front became the main one, and the offensive toward Marsa Matruh was never mentioned again.; the African front was considered stable while things were going very badly in Greece for Mussolini's troops; therefore on November 7, 1940 the Chief of General Staff Marshal Pietro Badoglio sent a telegram to Graziani summarizing the Italian strategic situation:

After the start of operations against Greece, the strategic line of war can be considered as follows:

1) from Albania air-ground offensive action for the full occupation of Greece;

2) from the Motherland, an aerial offensive action in conjunction with an offensive action 94 in Greece, especially directed against the enemy's land and naval installations;

3) from Libya air and ground actions limited to the conquest of Marsa Matruh, from where, then, firmly positioned to defend, carry out an active lively air action on the port of Alexandria to make life impossible for the English fleet;

4) in the Aegean defensive air - land - maritime action, aimed at maintaining possession and offensive air and naval action against the English and Greek fleets;

5) in the Empire, air-ground action intended essentially to last;

6) for the Navy to protect traffic with Albania and Northern Africa and naval forces in power to oppose any offenses by enemy forces.

From the above results:

- that the main operation to be carried out is that which has as its objective the integral occupation of Greece, which will absorb a large quantity of troops (from twenty to twenty-five divisions) and materials and will engage most of the naval, war and fees, to carry out transport and ensure connections;

- that operations in Egypt, with an objective limited to the occupation of Marsa Matruh, will have to be adapted to the new situation.

Following and confirmation of my comuniccation nr. 3542 Op on two current month, I therefore beg you, Excellency, to want to review your projects, adapting the requests to the new more limited operational requirements and keeping in mind that the start-up of vehicles indicated to you by the State Army Major with comunication 09600/341 on the current 1st month will not undergo variations as a result of the current situation. Also the operational projects relating to the Tunisian border (I refer to your letter nr. 01/1775 of 25 October) will have to be adequate to the limited means available for that board.

In vain Graziani stormed Badoglio for means and supplies:

(...) Please, Excellency, to ensure that the vessels prepared or in preparation in Naples are loaded as soon as possible on two or three special steamships and immediately diverted to Tripoli.

I remind you (and it is also lawful to do this when the supreme interest of the Fatherland, which you protect) is at stake, the cry that you sent me in your march on Addis Ababa, to which, making unprecedented efforts to meet you, I was not deaf for complete your victory which was only then totalitarian.

I send you General Giordano who is in charge of presiding over the boarding of the vehicles. He will be able to tell you everything you want to ask him without reservations on my part as I have always authorized to do by all the officers of S.M. sent readers of my documents. With this letter of mine I said my last word.

My effort cannot go beyond the limits of the possible, of humanity and of the most determined Will. I would not want to find myself at the tragic moment of having accomplished with enormous effort road and water, and still having to procrastinate for the rest. Then certainly the responsibility for events cannot fall solely on me in front of the homeland which alone is immortal.

He received nothing.

OPERATION COMPASS:
WAVELL'S OFFENSIVE

Hitler sent General Ritter von Thoma as an observer to the battlefield in early November, in part growing out of a German offer in September of two armored divisions to fight in Africa. Additionally, Hitler began to prepare the 3rd Panzer division for transfer to Africa. But von Thoma was not encouraged. Von Thoma came back feeling that Italian leadership was not up to snuff (he thought Graziani was poor as CinC), and the logistics, climate, and terrain were difficult. He did state that if German forces were committed, that it should be four divisions. More would be too difficult to support, and less than that could not complete the taskthis was a remarkable prediction that was probably accurate.

Some Germans saw support for a Mediterranean policy as a way to bring Britain to her knees. Both Admiral Erich Raeder of the *Kriegsmarine* and General Alfred Jodl supported this policy, yet, General Franz Halder, Chief of Staff of the *Oberkommando Der Wehrmacht* remarked on the Italian advance,

Italy's economic dependence and lack of organizational ability hinder a decisive Italian effort.

Hitler felt that the Mediterranean was secondary and would not have a decisive effect on bringing Britain to her knees. Marshal Badoglio hoped that the desolation of the desert would reinforce this feeling too, as the Italian army did not want Germans in their sphere. Equipment yes, but not with the troops. Thus, in a meeting between Mussolini and Hitler on 4 October 1940, Mussolini did admit that he might need heavy tanks, trucks, and divebombers to continue the third phase of the advance from Mersa Matruh to the Delta, but for now he did not want any German divisions. The ready to go 3. Panzer, even in desert camouflage paint, was assigned elsewhere.

After von Thoma's visit, Graziani gave some thought to concentrating vehicles and tanks into a division. But the most he ever implemented was a motorized force which, in part, was created due to the successful skirmishing of the British armored cars. This *raggruppamento*, akin to a reinforced regiment, or a special grouping of units at regimental strength or greater, became the Maletti Group.

Additionally, there was a key tactical error that the Italians committed. The troops were disposed in a series of armed camps, but they were not mutually supporting and there was not a strong mobile force that could be relied upon to halt any troops that might push through the gaps[8].

On the morning of November 19 General Gallina, commander of the Libyan Divisions, was informed that the air force had broken up enemy armored personnel carriers in Bir Enba and in the areas of Alam Abu Hileiuat about thirty kilometers south of Sidi el Barrani, and that mechanized units they were stationed northwest of Alam el Heilif; Gallina ordered that the two fast columns, moving respectively from the advanced positions of Alma el Tummar and Alam Nibeua, point to Alam Abu Heleiuat, with the task of exploring the area within a radius of three kilometers.

---

[8] Greene, Massignani 1994, pp.28 segg.

Italian infantry on the counterattack during a sandstorm
(Kurt Caesar, 1941. Author's collection).

The 2nd Libyan was to hold another column in reserve.
At 12.40 the Maletti column, which first arrived at Alam Abu Heleiuat and signaled to artillery shots and attacked by armored cars and tanks, engaged in a bitter duel with the British. Towards 13.00 came the column of the 2nd Libyan, who immediately intervened with fire, reacting to the opponent's attempt to wrap his hips. After a hard struggle, the British wards were rejected; however, during the return to the bases of the Italian units, they returned to the charge causing lively rearguard fights, resolved in favor of Gallina also for the intervention of a squadron of *Breda* Ba.65 fighters who carried out machine-guns attacks at low altitude. Simultaneously, a group of FIAT CR. 42 faced an enemy air force, managing to shoot down six *Gloster Gladiators* without any losses. The reserve column, sent by the 2nd Libyan Division, had also rushed.
Despite the Italian success, numerous flaws had emerged in the action: General Gallina

expressed himself very frankly:

> if these columns had the purpose of respecting the adversary, occasional patrolling within a radius of seven to eight kilometers and, therefore, in the areas between one large unit and the other would have been sufficient. If, on the other hand, their aim was to seek and engage in combat with British mechanized formations to capture and destroy their elements, they were not at all suitable, with the means they currently had, to achieve this end. In fact, the enemy opposed these columns - consisting, at best, of a mass of trucks carrying artillery and a low aliquot of wagons - faster, more powerful and better protected means supported by more mobile and longer arm artillery.

The Italian columns, at a given moment, or, because they arrive at the target, or because they are forced by the enemy action, however, to express their only positive characteristic (the firepower of medium and large caliber artillery mounted on the trucks of the autocolumns), they were forced to stop: but when they had to return to their respective positions, they were faced with the crisis of detachment and retreat. And the folding imposed, with the alternation of the brackets, the halving of the forces to face the enemy, which naturally doubled its aggressiveness.
Gallina wrote in the report to the Army command:

> In these combat actions it will shine, as it has so far shone, the ability and the value of our commanders and our men, but we will never be able to put to our credit a clear tangible success.

On the eve of the Operation *Compass*, the Italians, at least on paper, had huge forces gathered around and in front of Sidi el Barrani. The two Libyan Divisions were deployed in six entrenched camps (four in Nibeiwa, Tummar and in a place called Quota 90, all south of the coastal road, one in Maktila immediately north of the road and one east of Sidi el Barrani himself), the 4th Black Shirts Division *3 Gennaio* and in the field of Nibeiwa an *ad hoc* formation in all equivalent to a Division, the Maletti Group. In reserve there was a Division into four other entrenched camps around Bir Sofafi and Bir el Rabia, south west of Sidi el Barrani and along the southern edge of the ridge. Another Division was located south of the coastal road, between Buq Buq and Sidi el Barrani, and two more to the west, near Sollum, Sidi Omar and Capuzzo, across the Halfaya pass.
As regards armored vehicles, the Italian situation, on December 1st, was as follows:

- I and II Battailon M 11/39 tanks (of which 22 tanks are efficient out of 72);
- III Battailon M 13/40 tanks (37 tanks), at the time the best available in A.S .;
- 7 battalions L tanks (309 light tanks between L 33 and L 35).

The Italian defenses consisted of large strongpoints equipped with heavy and light artillery; but the strongpoints were not adequately connected to each other due to the lack of mobile forces that could stem any enemy penetration into a single strongpoint.
In reality, given the state of the Italian forces present in the area, objectively it was not possible to constitute a stronger defense. Graziani lacked the armored forces to maneuver the enemy, there were no vehicles to quickly move fresh reserve units to the critical

points of the deployment attacked by enemy mechanized forces, anti-tank guns were missing. The defensive arrangements were scattered in the area south of Barrani and in the desert since it was necessary to cover the south front from possible penetrations of armored forces at that point of the front.

The defensive tactical position in that region was substantially correct.

The main mistake was in the occupation itself of Sidi el Barrani, a location that lent itself poorly for a static defense, like the Italian one. The best solution would have been to fall back towards Sollum-Halfaia where there was an easily defensible promontory or to fall back into Cyrenaic territory and defend Bardia and especially Tobruk, the two Italian strongholds.

Might as well, therefore, do not attack at all in September 1940, or attack only the locality of Sollum (as was the main idea of Graziani in the operational memory of the twenty-nine of July). The idea, however, of a withdrawal in December 1940 was unthinkable, both because the withdrawal order could never have come from Mussolini would not, for reasons of prestige, give the withdrawal order and because even if by hypothesis it had been given, the Italian troops were on foot, and a retreat in the desert on foot would have led to an absolute defeat.

General O'Connor, as Greene and Massignani reamarked, organized an assault on the Italians, built around the Matilda tank, which would bring about a brilliant victory. Fighting alongside the 7th Armored division was the 4th Indian division. The 4th represented the unbloodied cream of the Army of India that had been trained for years, and many of its units had served on the northwest frontier of India. British Guards units were available here too, while the comparable Italian formation, the elite *Granatieri di Sardegna* Division, remained in Italy. The armor was well trained, and they had a heavy tank, the *Matilda*, which the Italians, like the Germans at Arras in 1940, could not face, and like the Germans at Arras, could only run from. All of these troops had been trained through the interwar period as a tough professional core group, and even with the war expansion under way had not yet been diluted. Under one of the best British commanders of World War II, the ingredients were there for an Italian disaster, and so it transpired[9]

O'Connor had about 40,000 men ready for the attack: the 4th Indian Division, the 7th Armored Division and a formation known as *Selby Force*, comprising three mobile infantry columns, a tank department and some campaign cannons and light anti-aircraft 1,750 men in all who had been part of the Marsa Matruh garrison, under the command of Brigadier General A.R. Selby. The command of the Western Desert Force was in Maaten Bagush, on the coast, about 40 km east of Marsa Matruh. Maitland Wilson moved there during the first week of December and O'Connor, with his Chief of staff, brigadier general John Harding, set off on 6 December with his own troops.

In addition, the 6th *Australian Division*, consisting of the 16th and 17 th *Australian Infantry Brigade*, the 16th *Infantry Brigade* (detached from the 4th Indian Division) and the 7th RTR (detached from the 7th *Armored Division*) and the *Selby Force* (by the strength of a brigade).

The approach march in the first two days was almost 100 km of uncovered land without vegetation was accomplished during the day and by two Divisions with hundreds of vehicles without the Italians having any inkling. For two nights these forces camped in

---

[9]Green, Massignani 1994, p. 31.

the desert, about 16 km west of Bir el Kenayis, on the Marsa Matruh- Siwa Oasis road. Then, on the afternoon of Sunday 8 December, protected by low clouds that made Italian aerial reconnaissance difficult, they moved to the collection area located in the desert immediately south of Maktila and about 90 km west of the Marsa Matruh- Siwa Oasis road, at 17 the troops were all assembled. Until now the two Divisions had proceeded together, during the night between 8 and 9 December they separated and the 7th Armored pointed even further west, to be able to operate on a wider area, behind the Italian entrenched fields, at south of the road between Sidi el Barrani and Buq Buq.

The initial attack on the entrenched camps of Nibeiwa and Tummar was to be launched by the 4th *Indian Division*, coming from the west. The *Selby Force*, which left Marsa Matruh on 9 December, heading west along the road, was to block Maktila and press towards Sidi el Barrani himself.

On December 10 the garrison of Sidi el Barrani (1st Libyan Division and 4th *3 Gennaio* Black Shirt Division) was surrounded.

As this last stage was completed, the British navy with the powerfully armed monitor *Terror* and the two gunboats *Aphis* and *Ladybird*, with minor armament, began to cannon Sidi el Barrani and Maktila. Until about midnight the Italians in Nibeiwa remained on the living side, there were rather lively exchanges of rifle-making and rockets were launched. A little before 5 o'clock a Battailon of the 4th *Indian Div*. Temporarily detached, opened fire on the entrenched field from the east and subsequently attracted the attention of the enemy. This went on for almost an hour, after which an illusory quiet ensued. At 7.15 am the 72 divisional artillery guns began a short, intense bombing from the east. Within ten minutes the tanks of the 7th *Royal Tank* Rgt. swept away the northwest corner of the entrenched camp, knocking out about 25 medium and light Italian tanks parked outside the fortified wall. Two squadrons of *Matilda* MKII infantry tanks immediately entered the fight, engaging artillery and Italian infantry at a short distance. General Maletti, commander of the Group of the same name, was killed by a cannon shot from a tank while he was leaving his tent, shooting with a MAB 38.

Two infantry battalions of the 4th *Indian Division* passed through the breach almost immediately, the first of the 6th *Rajputana Rifles* and the second of the *Cameron Highlanders* Regiment, which attacked the Italians by force: the fight was fierce but within two hours the entrenched camp was in British hands. Meanwhile the 5th Indian Infantry Brigade (the 1st *Royal Fusiliers*, the 3rd / 1st *Punjabi Rifles* Regiment and the 4th Battailon of the 6th *Rajputana Rifles*) and one of the Division's artillery regiments moved over a wide arch west to Nibeiwa, to prepare for attack the next target, West Tummar. Further west, on an even wider arc, the 7th *Armored Division* was advancing from the dawn, the 4th *Armored Brigade* at the head, aiming without finding resistance on the coastal road about 56 km from the starting line. Before 11 am the tanks had completed their task in Nibeiwa and could leave the final task to the *Rajputana* and *Cameron* riflemen.

Lt. Col. G. R. Stevens of the 4th *Indian Division* remember:

> Frightened, dazed, or desperate Italians erupted from tents and slit trenches, some to surrender supinely, others to leap gallantly into battle, hurling grenades or blazing machine guns in futile belabour of the impregnable intruders.

The Black Shirts from Sicily and Puglia fought strenuously, and even when the Italian defense collapsed and yielded the strongpoints of the *3 Gennaio*; the Black Shirts resisted until the night the assault of the 16th British Brigade (belonging to the 4th *Indian Division*) until complete annihilation allowing the Italian units to fall back. Only on 11 December the bulletin of the Supreme Command n. 187 communicated the news of the British offensive, announcing the death of General Maletti; the *3 Gennaio* Division and the 1st Libyan were mentioned, for the heroic behavior:

While fighting in the Sidi el Barrani region, at the Divisions still in Marmarica, 1st and 2nd Black Shirt Division *23 Marzo* and *28 Ottobre*, were given orders to organize to defend themselves on the Halfaya ridge line.

Enemy armored vehicles overlooked the southernmost border, at Garn ul Grein and Sidi Omar, hinting at a wide-ranging encirclement to cut communications between Bardia and Tobruk. As a consequence of this, the Higher Command A.S. he ordered:

- at 11 am on 12 December: that the 2nd CC.NN. *28 Ottobre* was intended to guard the Piazza di Bardia;
- at 16: that the Black Shirt Divisions 1st *23 Marzo* and 2nd *28 Ottobre* must pass to the disposal of the XXIII C.A. (General Bergonzoli);
- at 19: that the four Divisions *23 Marzo*, *28 Ottobre*, *Marmarica* and *Cirene* all passed under the orders of General Bergonzoli.

On 14 December 1940 there was strong pressure from the British armored vehicles on the strongpoints of *28 Ottobre* on the Halfaya line. Following the increased threat of circumvention, the 2nd Division CC.NN. received the order to fall back on Bardia.

December 15, 1940 the British unleashed violent attacks by armored vehicles against March 23 in Bir ci Tafua, near Bardia-

While still fighting in Sidi el Barrani and on the Halfaya, the British began storming Bardia from above with the *Royal Air Force*.

The objectives of the RAF were above all the residential area and the warehouses. Continued aerial bombardments followed on defense works, and on workers.

Bombings were also carried out from the sea, on 17, 18, 19 December, then on 31 and 1 January. The encirclement was completed on December 20, then the offensive bets of reconnaissance of the defenses and then those of tasting began.

Bardia was abandoned to herself with her garrison while the Special Armored Brigade that protected the way to Tobruk already infested by the explorers of the *Long Range Desert Group* tried to keep a road open. It was therefore the turn of Sidi el Barrani which fell on December 15th. The artillery in a position war is the only one capable of fighting the enemy effectively. Once identified by the observers, however, the position was easily beaten by the counterbattery shot which, unlike the Italian artillery, could easily move. Once the ammunition was exhausted, all that was left was to undermine the fire mouths to avoid reuse. The 7th *Armored*'s units had meanwhile made contact with the *Cirene* and *Catanzaro* Divisions which, protected by artillery, retreated to Sollum and the Halfaya pass.

The British lined up MKVI light tanks equipped with machine guns, technically inferior to the M11 / 39, and *Cruiser* tanks armed with a 40 mm cannon which, excluding the revolving turret, had the same offensive capacity as the M11 / 39 tanks. The M13 / 40 tank was already on African territory, armed with the 47/32 piece, in a revolving turret but was not yet being distributed to the units or was running in. On 14/12, after a sandstorm, the Italian *Regia Aeronautica* managed to resume flights and inflict numerous losses on the enemy. According to the plan, the operation could be considered concluded but General O'Connor, an excellent commander, who wore on his chest the ribbon of the Italian Silver Medal for Military Bravery and Military Cross won at Vittorio Veneto battle in 1918, evaluating the possibility of the situation he decided to continue in Libyan territory. Thus fell Sollum, Sidi Omar and the reduced Capuzzo.

The general Annibale Bergonzoli, commander of the XXIII Army Corps entrenched in Bardia with 4 Divisions, including the 2nd Black Shirt Division *28 Ottobre*.

The siege of Bardia began on December 20th and will last for three weeks. The defensive wall developed for 33 kilometers and had an anti-tank moat, minefields, barbed wire. Meanwhile, the Italian Supreme Command thought back to the German proposal made 2 months earlier (about sending two Panzerdivisions to Libya, whose urgency was now evident to everyone. Graziani himself had now fallen out of favor with Mussolini.

On December 20, Marshal Badoglio sent a letter to Graziani in which he wished him a quick victory against the enemy. Marshal of Italy Rodolfo Graziani thus replied to Badoglio:

> Too late! Your solidarity, Marshal Badoglio, had to give it to me first when you did nothing to support my efforts to make understand the impossibility of the Egyptian enterprise with the means with which it was available.

Bardia
(Kurt Caesar, 1941. Author's collection)

THE FALL OF BARDIA

The responsibility for the defense of Bardia fell to the commander of the XXIII Army Corps, Annibale Bergonzoli, whose moves it is useful to summarize after the British offensive. We will therefore take a step back to follow its moves.

In Sidi el Barrani, under British pressure, Bergonzolia had proceeded to withdraw. However, he did not fail to proceed with an intense covering fire of his artillery, hoping to mask the simultaneous release. In this way the *Cirene* and *Marmarica* Divisions reached Bardia on the coast and Ridotta Capuzzo respectively at Sollum.

The withdrawal was carried out in a disciplined and orderly manner, except having to abandon a lot of material on the previous positions, including some ammunition reserves and several artillery guns, which were considered inefficient. The frenzied expectation of the enemy became feverish, so much so that the pause was understood by Bergonzoli as the best way to consolidate the retreat and close himself inside Bardia's defensive belt. Meanwhile, the untimely Berti had returned to Libya; these, before endorsing his subordinate's curbing decisions, asked Graziani to weigh up the situation on the ground. For a prompt response, given that Graziani had full confidence in the commander of the XXIII Corps, he bitterly defended Bergonzoli, judging him in full conscience capable of assessing the risks and opportunities: if Bergonzoli had decided to reach Bardia, it meant that no other solution was possible. In short, Graziani understood that the real risk for the XXIII Corps was the opposing encirclement, an event to be avoided in any way, if the goal for the Italian deployment was to ensure the constant connection between the center and the periphery at any cost.

On December 15, Graziani ordered Bergonzoli to defend Bardia and Tobruk indefinitely, in order to stop the British advance. Aware of the great task entrusted to him, Bergonzoli began major renovations of the stronghold: he increased the efficiency of the 37 km long perimeter line, created a protective system of mines, cleared the modest anti-tank ditch completely full of sand. No less attention was paid to the logistical aspect, in anticipation of a long siege: the distribution of water and food was reduced.

In the meantime, O'Connor withdrew the 7th Armored Brigade beyond Bardia, which received and sold units, for its strengthening in view of the pursuit of the Italians in the Cyreneic Jebel.

From January 1, 1941, the Western Desert Force became the 13th Army Corps.

With the aid of security fighters and armored vehicles, the 16th Australian Inf. Brigade attacked the welding of the Gerfan and Ponticelli sectors; the British managed to overcome the anti-tank ditch and the latticework, forcing the passage between the cornerstones Bu Rim and Garridia, blossomed on the second position and divided into two masses; the first towards Gerfan and the second, stronger, towards Ponticelli, subsequently eliminating the welding target of Marmarica and taking on the reverse the second line held by the battalions of the 115th and 116th Infantry Regiments and the battery posts.

As soon as he heard of the failure of the two right-hand strongpoints of the *Ponticelli* sector defended by the I / 116th infantry, General Bergonzoli ordered the commander of the 116th infantry to prepare a counterattack, sending him a tank company M 13/40, some 47/ 132 guns and 20 mm MG and the Commander of the *28 Ottobre* to send the CXXXV Black Shirts Battalion, two batteries of 75/27 guns, and the LX Battailon Light Tanks (12) to the Ponticelli sector, at the disposal of the Army Corps. L3 tankettes).

The CXXXV Battalion CC.NN. and the two batteries of the *28 Ottobre* were deployed to block the valley and the Uadi el Garridia rolling stock.

On the *23 Marzo*'s front, after a useless and bloody resistance, the cornerstone and the artillery of Bu Rim where the CXVIII Black Shirts Battalion fought; continued to fight. Meanwhile at 12 noon the entire 116th *Treviso* Infantry Rgt (div. *Marmarica*) was completely and definitively overwhelmed. At the late hours of the same day 3 the *Ponticelli* sector was almost entirely in the power of the enemy; in the Garfan sector, the 23 Marzo lost the strongpoint and the artillery deploied at Bu Rim and the stronghold Scegheila was shocked by the fire.

The *28 Ottobre* was deployed on the positions of the Uadi el Hereiga and his CXXXV Black Shirts Battalion fought in the Uadi el Garridia area and cemetery of Bardia.

On the morning of January 4, while fighting continued in the *Ponticelli* sector against battalions II and III of the 115th *Marmarica* Infantry Regiment, invested by the Australian brigades XVI and XIX, supported by numerous tanks, and in the Mrega sector the Australians always supported by the tanks, after strenuous struggle they managed to occupy the cornerstones held by the I / 158th and III / 157th *Liguria* Infantry (*Cirene* Division) while the survivors lined up to defend the wadi at quote 145.

British artillery bombarded Italian positions incessantly as enemy mechanized vehicles attacked and were repelled; the British diverted and headed for Bardia.

The last men of the 2nd Division *28 Ottobre* will continue the resistance until 16.15. they surrendered only after a strenuous and uneven struggle.

Even the tank crews fought fiercely, right down to the last man.

The other two Divisions of *Black Shirts* ceased to exist, fighting until the last, unlike others, too many others italian troops. Of the entire *28 Ottobre* Division remained only one Battailon, the CXL, joined to the *Sirte* Division and which was lost in Tobruk.

Still from Ciano's Diary:

> JANUARY 5 - Bardia's radio is silent from 4 pm yesterday. We only receive news through British press releases. The resistance of our troops was short: a matter of hours. Yet there was no shortage of weapons. There were only 430 guns. Why didn't the fight last longer? Still the flea fight against the elephant? "Singular flea" says Mussolini who had more than a thousand cannons between Sidi el Barrani, Bardia and Tobruk. One day I will have to decide to empty the bag and tell the whole truth to the Italians stunned by too many lies. After January 3, I will make February 3: a speech by those who whip in blood. (...)

The fall of the Cyrenaic stronghold was announced to the Italians with the war bulletin number 214 of January 7:

> The last stronghpoints that still resisted in Bardia fell towards the evening of the 5th. Our troops have, for 25 days, written sublime pages of daring and inflicted heavy losses on the enemy. Ours were also strong, in materials, in men: fallen, wounded, missing.

In Bardia the Italians lost 1,703 dead, 3,740 injured and 36,000 prisoners, the British

130 dead and 326 injured.

Regards the British strategic situation in the Middle East, we can read what was written by Winston Churchill to General Wavell on January 6, 1941, the day after the fall of Bardia:

> The present composition of the Army in the Middle East (excluding almost 120,000 from Kenya and Aden) therefore amounts to 150,000 men of combat troops.
>
> Follow 40,000 men of the troop assigned to the lines of communication and 20,000 to the bases, and elsewhere ... that is, 150,000 plus 60,000. To these will be added the 22,000 fighters and 17,000 of another kind, transported by the W.S.5 convoy. so there will be a total of 172,000 fighters and 77,000 employed in the rear.
>
> The WS6 convoy, now under load, contains 8,500 fighter planes plus 4,000 recruits, a part of which, say 2,500, brings the total number of fighters to 11,000, excluding the mobile naval base, composed of 5,300 men, the RAF and the Navy, with 7,000 men, 2,000 free French and around 9,000 of other services.
>
> After the arrival of this convoy, the total forces in the Middle East will include 183,000 fighters and 85,000 service workers: that is, there will be a proportion of 15 to 7.
>
> At this point the progressive worsening in the proportion between fighting troops and rear services should be noted. I deeply regret the resulting composition of the Middle East. When all these convoys have arrived, the total of the men transported by it will amount to 240,000 plus 43,000 plus 20,000 altogether over 300,000 to which must be added the 70,000 in Kenya.
>
> Total: 370,000 men to pay and feed.

Against them were the 340,000 men of the Duke of Aosta - of whom 91,000 Italians - in East Africa and the 207,917 who remained to Graziani after the loss of Sidi el Barrani and Bardia, in addition to the French troops loyal to the government of Vichy in Lebanon and Syria, about 33,000 men.

In Bardia the Italians lost 1,703 dead, 3,740 wounded and 36,000 prisoners, the British 130 dead and 326 wonded.

The next British target was Tobruk.

Here, after a violent attack at 7.15 am on 21 January 1941 with tanks against the clearly rejected Ras Medauar stronghold, the British - protected by smoke and with the mass of the tanks - invested the cornerstones Dahar el Azazi and Bir Junes of the eastern sector and they managed to open a gap between the two cornerstones; it was 7.30. After the tanks, Australian infantry burst into the gate before the 16th and then the 19th Infantry Brigade, on brent carriers and on foot trucks and mixed with other tanks. The enemy forces were immediately fanned, left, middle and right of the deployment of our artillery, opening the way to other mechanized units of the 6th Australian Infantry Division.

By stifling the residual resistance, the Australians came to the crossroads of El Adem, a key position in the entire defense system.

Despite everything, the Italians resisted. A counterattack of M 11/39 tanks and motorized troops of the reserve forced the British, already arrived in the area between the *Piave* and q 144 strongpoints, to temporarily fall back .

At 13.30, however, all resistance was eliminated and the stronghold of El Adem was already in the hands of the enemy; some of the tank crewmen managed to hold out until 15.30.

On 22 and 23 January all the other centers and strongholds, togheter with isolated batteries of the Army and the Navy, fell: In the general collapse, the Black Shits of the Volontari della Libia Battalion were also overwhelmed. The Fascist Militia had ceased to exist in Cyrenaica.

Bergonzoli had asked Graziani to the end for a sortie from Tobruk or a flanking action of his own air force, but nothing was done. The Royal Air Force waged its own war and since the new Chief of General Staff Cavallero was engaged in Albania, Cyrenaica had in fact been abandoned to its fate. or.

After the fall of Bardia Bergonzoli had reached Tobruk, and after the fall of this stronghold he managed to reach the Italian lines; proceeded at night, to remain hidden during the day, always under the pressure of the British.

Now reconnected with his own lines, he was transferred to Derna, where the new commander of the 10th Army Tellera entrusted Bergonzoli with a further desperate task: to attempt a new obstruction to the British ramp. The strength assigned to him was very low and below the hierarchical level of the army corps, which he would have been able to hold: a total of 5,000 heterogeneous collected men. The mission was impossible, but not unusual for a guy like Bergonzoli, who accepted with his usual enthusiasm. Morale, however, was starting to drop, given that on Via Balbia and inland, the towns fell one after the other into British hands.

So it was that in early February Bergonzoli's task was to facilitate the retreat of the 20th Army Corps, which attempted to reach Benghazi and Agedabia from the top of the Cyreneic cliff. He still had some mobility, having columns of tanks; however, it was not prudent to go into the desert. The British, who proceeded by winding, would have easily surrounded any isolated formation. Bergonzoli thus moved westward, using whatever means at his disposal: he first reached Barce and then Benghazi.

The British realized that there were more troops in Tobruk than previously thought: about 30,000 men, including numerous specialists and a naval detachment of more than 2,000 men. Here too there were so many vehicles that nobody bothered to count them, 87 tanks and more than 200 guns. There was a large fuel depot and 10,000 tons of water in the tank, canned food, fruit, vegetables and meat, which had not been distributed to the troops.

An attempt was made to put the port out of commission but the Royal Navy had already refitted it 48 hours after the Italian surrender. The losses of the XIII army corps were slightly higher than 400 men, 355 of which were Australians.

On the day the assault against Tobruk was launched the British chiefs of staff informed Wavell that the capture of Benghazi was now considered of great importance. O'Connor was already making plans for this other leap forward. He had ordered that the 7th Armored Brigade continue to advance towards Derna and that the 4th Armored Brigade begin to march on El Mechili, 160 kilometers away. On the evening of January 22 the first was in contact with the Italians, 30 kilometers from Derna, while patrols of the second were already on the slopes leading from El Mechili to the west, south and south east.

The commander of the 10th Army, General Tellera attempted to create an articulated defense on the Derna-Berta-el Mechili line. It should have stopped the main enemy effort with the static resistance of the stronger north wing and with the maneuver of moving elements south in the desert. This task was entrusted to the 25,000 men of the 10th army, deployed on the 120 km. In Tellera, all that remained was to have his troops clinging to the plateau of the Cyrenaic Jebel.

In Derna, in order to block the Via Balbia Tellera, it concentrated 5000 men, including the *Sabratha* Division; it was a heterogeneous force, coming from different units, including the Libyan paratrooper Battailon, composed of excellent personnel, with artillery of various caliber, which placed under the orders of Bergonzoli miraculously emerged from the siege of Bardia. In Mechili - little more than an isolated outpost - he left the armored brigade Babini. Within a static cordon defense, this centralized force should have given a sense of dynamism and reaction, in order to lessen any opponent's attack. However, the problem was in the morphology of the desert terrain, devoid of large tactical holds in Mechili.

Regardless of this, the defence line was renamed by Graziani himself in a high-sounding way as the *Grappa of Libya*.

On the evening of January 23, all that remained of the army that Graziani had at his disposal at the beginning of December was the Sabratha Division (minus an infantry regiment) in position immediately east of Derna, an armored brigade of about 160 tanks, and the other infantry regiment of the 60th Division which was in El Mechili under the orders of General Babini. Further west, it was not known for certain whether there were two other Divisions in Cyrenaica or Tripolitania. The northern core of the forces in Cyrenaica held the coastal road that went to Benghazi while the southern core was attested on the main junction between the communication routes coming from the desert, from the Jebel and from the coast. Wavell saw clearly as O'Connor the possibility of a rapid advance on Benghazi and a decisive victory. O'Connor accomplished both goals in less than three weeks. The pace of this final phase of the campaign was frenetic.

While the 6th Australian Inf. Division was arrested in Derna by the *Sabratha* Division assisted by the Libyan paratrooper Battailon, the 7th Armored reached el Mechili, a crossroads of strategically important runways within the Cyreneic Jebel.

If Mechili had fallen, the entire Cyrenaic front would have been circumvented on the desert side and therefore the troops of the 10th Army would have been forced to another retreat to avoid the encirclement.

The 4th *Armored Brigade* included the 3th *Hussars* with 25 MkVI and 9 *Cruisers*, the 7th Hussars with 26 MkVI and 1 Cruiser, the 2nd RTR with 6 MkVI and 21 Cruisers (3 A9t anks, 7 A10, 11 A13) for a total of 57 MkVI and 31 Cruiser.

The Italians lined up the *Babini Armored Brigade*, with light and medium tanks, artillery and the 10th *Bersaglieri* Regiment, with *Piana Motorized Group* and the *Bignami Column* in reserve.

The *Babini Armored Brigade* had 138 officers, 2,200 non-commissioned officers and troops, 8 guns of 75/27,8 of 100/17, 8 guns of 47/32 and 16 of 20/65, 12 machine guns Fiat 35, 4 of 12, 7mm, 7 *Solothurn* anti-tank shooters, 6 81mm mortars, 57 M 13/40 tanks, 25 HP33, 6 AB40 armored cars, 30 flamethrowers, 90 light and 160 heavy trucks, 180 motorcycles;

the *Piana Motorized Group* included 121 officers, 2,241 troopers, 12 cannons of 105/28 and 24 of 75/27, 12 guns of 65/17, 20 of 20/65, 62 machine guns Fiat 35, 18 Brixia mortars of 45, 10 flamethrowers, 115 light trucks, 83 heavy trucks, 120 motorcycles.

The *Bignami Column* framed the XXV ° and XXVII ° Motorized Machine Gun Battailon, a group of 12 guns of 75/27 detached from the 10th Artillery Regiment of the div. *Bologna*, VI and XXI M13 / 40 Battailons , each out of 37 tanks.

The clashes of El Mechili took place between 24 and 25 January 1941. In a first phase the British MkVI, light tanks armed with 12.7mm machine guns, came to be under attack by medium tanks suffering some losses: the majority of sources say at least five British tanks destroyed. Following this unexpected Italian counter-offensive, the British light tanks withdrew. In the second phase, the British counterattacked bringing other vehicles to the front line, such as the 2pdr portee and some 25pdr to support the cruiser tanks, armed with a 2pdr cannon, capable of piercing the armor of the Italian tanks. . The British lost an A10 cruiser and another MkVI in addition to many others damaged for a total of 20-25 vehicles hit. In difficulty because of this new clash, the British again retreated, chased by the Italians who, however, ended up under the fire of the 2pdr portee and the 25 pdr, losing between 4 and 6 medium tanks; furthermore, Babini's tanks had lost radio contact with the base and therefore went back. O'Connor decided to crush what remained of the Italian forces in this area by facing the *Sabratha* Division in Derna, which together with the Libyan paratroopers had blocked the Australians, delaying British plans.

On February 25, after ten days of fierce fighting, the Libyan infantrymen were overwhelmed by the Australians in el Fteiah, and forced to yield ground, then being surrounded by British motorized units; of the entire *Tonini Group,* only 148 officers, non-commissioned officers and paratroopers survived, who managed to fall back.

Due to the resistance of the *Sabratha* O'Connor was therefore forced to leave two brigades of the 6th *Australian Infantry Division* near Derna, and sent the third brigade south to join the 7th Armored Division and the support group. On January 25 he gave explicit orders to inhibit General Babini and his troops from withdrawing from El Mechili.

Most of these forces, however, were blocked by a lack of fuel until the morning of January 27 and overnight, Babini had escaped the encirclement by heading north. When the aerial reconnaissance discovered the Italians on a road that did not appear in any English map, they quickly departed or the 4th *Armored Brigade* launched their pursuit for two days, and the fighter-bombers attacked them with machine-gun fire and with light bombs. But on the afternoon of January 28, things went very badly: heavy rain, numerous mechanical breakdowns and fuel shortages forced the hunting to be stopped.

On January 29 the Italians withdrew from Derna. Australians occupied Derna on January 30th. O'Connor thought for a moment that he could give some of his officers and men some breathing space and be able to put the tanks and worn-out material back on track. To wrap the enemy on the Jebel, it was necessary to make the 7th Armored Division perform a movement wider than the simple approach march along the track that led from El Mechili to the west.

During the following two days the Italian resistance on the front held by the Australians, in the northern sector, began to decrease considerably due to the release of the troops and news came that the *Regia Aeronautica* was abandoning the few fields still occupied by it, moving back to Tripolitania.

In the early hours of the morning these rumors of folding found confirmation when long moving columns west of Barce and tanks were stocked which, again in Barce, were loaded onto trains. On the evening of January 31, during a meeting with his generals O'Connor he claimed that the Italians were preparing to abandon not only the coastal sector but the entire Cyrenaica. Maximum speed was essential in the pursuit: he could not afford to wait for reinforcements that would not have reached him before 10 February.

The next morning at the urgent request of O'Connor, Dorman Smith flew to Cairo from the commander in chief to obtain authorization for a rapid advance in order to intercept the Italian retreat.

Only then did the *Duce*, also due to the ongoing crisis on the Albanian front, decide to ask Hitler for the help he had previously refused. In the exposition of the Führer on the political and military situation held in Berchtesgaden on January 20, 1941, and sent to the Italian General Staff, it is evident the final decision to send German armored troops to Libya.

German units were therefore preparing to intervene in Libya: in the meantime Graziani would have to resist as long as possible, waiting for Germanic aid, which would only come in the second half of February.

Asking the Germans for help led to a loss of prestige for Italy and the end of the parallel war.

A first reference to Germanic aid to the Italians in Libya dates back to September 3, 1940, when between the Italian military officer in Berlin, General Marras, and General Jodl of the OKW, mention was made of German units to be sent to Libya. A month later, on 4 October, Mussolini and Hitler met at the Brenner Pass and the matter was resumed, as already mentioned; Mussolini refused, thanking, the sending of German troops claiming that the only things that could be needed are trucks, a rate of heavy tanks and some formations of Stukas.

In this context, General Ritter von Thoma's visit to Libya took place, which took place in late October 1940.

Von Thoma made his visit almost close to the attack on Greece. In his report to Hitler, Von Thoma pointed out the serious shortcomings of the Italian armed forces in Libya: shortages of vehicles, tanks and inadequate individual equipment. The general's suggestion was to send an expeditionary force over 4 armored Divisions, the maximum number that could be successfully replenished in Libya. Sending such an expeditionary force to Libya would undoubtedly have allowed the Germans to definitively defeat Wavell's men. In fact, if the Western Desert Force appeared to be able to cope with the Italians, not so much could be said if it had immediately found itself facing the Germans.

At this stage of the conflict, Italy and Germany, although united in the war against England, were particularly keen to preserve their spheres of influence. A possible German intervention in A.S.I. he found a different welcome among the Italians: Mussolini would have accepted it as long as his weight was not preponderant and did not disfigure the Italians, preferring to continue fighting his parallel war.

Badoglio and Graziani instead strongly opposed direct intervention.

In Germany, in the OKW the opinions on the sending of a German contingent

British tanks and infantrymen at Beda Fomm
(Kurt Caesar, 1941. Author's collection)

FOX KILLED IN THE OPEN.
THE BATTLE OF BEDA FOMM

In the meantime, the 7th Armored Division, without waiting for any reinforcement, had moved forward on O'Connor's order to continue until he had a chance to move. As far as supplies were concerned, the first convoys loaded in Tobruk were starting to arrive in El Mechili and by February 4 the Division could have proceeded with its vehicles complete with supplies and be followed by a convoy with fuel water, supplies and ammunition needed for two days. All this complex had already received the notice to be ready to move on Msus. On February 4, Wavell himself flew to Cyrenaica. Returning to Cairo earlier in the night, he informed the Imperial Chief of Staff that what remained of the 7th Armored Division, a brigade with 40-50 heavy tanks and about 80 light tanks and the support group, whose vehicles were worn out and whose men exhausted he was aiming for Msus that he could have reached in the evening. At the same time the Australians were advancing along the main road to Barce and Benghazi and the RAF beat the retreating Italians. British tanks occupied Msus that same day but the proven 7th Armored Division was struggling to advance in that rugged region and only at dawn on February 5 could it report being in position east of Msus.
The chase continued throughout the day. The 4th *Armored Brigade* was approaching Beda Fomm where the Italians were hurrying together for what could have been their last stance.
At 10.30 on February 6, 1941, the bulk of the Italian forces that tried to reach Agedabia by abandoning the Cyrenaica now almost completely occupied by the British, were irremediably blocked by enemy armored units at the height of the Arab *marabout*, 39 kilometers from Agedabia.
The immense folding column was hit on the side by artillery fire while dozens of tanks and armored cars enveloped the formation's head, preventing it from moving. The strategic plan worked out by Wavell was perfectly successful. While the 6th *Australian Division* occupied Benghazi and later followed the rear guards of the 10th Army, who retreated along the coastal road, the 7th *Armored*, pushed from Derna into the desert, circumvented the Jebel Achdar, occupied el-Mechili and continued his difficult marches on infamous tracks reaching Msus on February 4, Antelat on the 5th and the Mediterranean coast the following day, closing Italian forces in a trap without escape. As the correspondent of *the Times* recounts,

> No army had ever crossed such a vast land before. In order to accomplish the feat it had been necessary to reduce the ration of water to just one glass a day, and everything had been sacrificed at speed, even the stops for meals and for night rest.

To complete the encirclement of Italian forces, British engineers had sprinkled the Via Balbia with mines, making it impractical. It should also be said that while the motorized and armored English units could maneuver freely on all the terrain surrounding the road, the Italian ones, mounted on vehicles, were tied to the rolling stock and were easy targets

A column of 5,000 men, comprising mainly artillerymen with their guns but also several civilian refugees, surrendered south west of Beda Fomm. O'Connor transferred his advanced command to Msus and at dawn on February 6 it was clear to the British that the Italians were preparing to make one last attempt to open a way in the circle that had quickly formed around them. The troops of the 10th Army fought with true fury and valor all day but when the evening came their situation was desperate.

On the morning of February 6, General Babini still had 16 officers and 2300 men, 24 chariots of the V Battailon and 12 of the III, in the rear, 24 artillery guns, 18 anti-tank guns, 320 trucks and other minor vehicles. The decisive moment arrived, at 1 pm on that day, about fifty kilometers from Agedabia, the M 13/40s of the 5th Battailon collided with British armored personnel arriving from the east. The third Battailon intervened to help them; the British, folding, lost three tanks and left prisoners. At 4 pm the tanks of the III Btl., supported by the batteries of the 12th Artillery, successfully intervened again in aid of another column of the 10th Army attacked by about twenty English tanks. During the movement of the Army, many columns had meanwhile remained trapped between Beda Fomm and the sea. About twenty British Cruiser tanks block the pace. After fierce fighting, only four M 13/40 of the VIth Battalion, which fell into the ambush of the British *Cruisers*, were saved. The VIth Medium Tanks Battailon was destroyed, it was formed by the 33rd Armoured Regiment of Parma, passed to the deposit of the 32nd Regiment of Verona and landed in Libya only on 22 January. The tanks of the XXI Battailon, arrived too late and cut off from a field undermined in the meantime by the enemy, they failed to contribute to the offensive effort. .

Lieutenant Norman Plow of the 2nd RTR later wrote about the Italian tactic that

> [Italian tactics] were poor - simply frontal attacks against our highest positions. Instead of attacking us with at least 50 tanks that could have overwhelmed us, they advanced slowly with small groups of 15 or 20. For us they were fairly easy shooting exercises (it was fairly early gunnery pratices for us).

The commander of the 10th Army, Giuseppe Tellera, also fell in combat.

> Tellera was among the casualties, mortally wounded. He had made a gallant effort and had failed. Such is the fortune of war.

General Tellera regardless of the strong fire, got into one of the surviving tanks and tried to go up the column to meet General Bergonzoli's armored brigade and with this make the last attempt to break the encirclement. But as he climbed up the deployment he collided with an enemy armored formation and was seriously injured in a lung. In a letter dated May 31, 1941, Medical Lieutenant Mauro Sabiani described the General's last hours to his wife as follows:

> His Excellency had several grenade splinter wounds in several parts of the body, the most serious of which was a lung penetration to the third right intercostal space. He had been hit by a sliver of grenade that had burst him a few meters away. [...] He suffered, breathed badly, and found it difficult to speak. [...] The General died in my arms at two o'clock on February 7 in the Cyrenaic desert, near Solluch. May it be comforting, lady, to know that your dear husband was never touched by a hand that was not Italian: for my pride and my duty. [...] Meanwhile, the English High Commanders, who had evidently

been made aware of the fact, personally authorized me to accompany the body to Benghazi and had me accompanied by an Anglican chaplain captain.

Tellera was the only Army Commander who died fighting in either the two world wars in the world. He received the Golden Medal for Military Bravery in memory with the following motivation:

> Chief of Staff of the High Command of the Armed Forces of Northern Africa, he was an active and provident organizer, especially in the period that led our weapons to the victory of Sidi El Barrani. Assumed, in a particularly critical situation, the command of an army he retained the most serene calm during the forced retreat from the Cyrenaic Jebel giving bright proofs of high command ability and eminent personal value. In the battle of South Bengasino, when the enemy had already made it impossible for our troops to retreat to Agedabia, in two days of bitter struggle, he stopped the opponent's impetuosity and inflicted serious losses, forcing him to desist from his push in Sirtica .
> Gathering the surviving troops in extreme defense in a particularly important location, he repeatedly tried, with serious personal risk, to gather the last means to break through and break the enemy encirclement. In this supreme heroic attempt he fell gloriously on the field, worthily, sealing a life of whole dedication to the Homeland.
>
> - Sidi El Barrani - Northern Africa September 1940 - Agedabia January 6, 1941.

Tellera was the only Army Commander of any Army fallen fighting in the two world wars. He received the Golden Medal for Military Valor in memory.

Along the thirty kilometers of the only possible way out, from Solluch to Agedabia the 7th A*rmored Division* managed to immobilize a chaotic mass of vehicles and men. In repeated attempts to open a breach, the Italians lost more than 80 tanks. Meanwhile O'Connor ordered the 6th *Australian Infantry Division* to send a swift detachment of the strength of about one brigade along the main road from Barce to Benghazi and on Ghemines to complete the encirclement of the Italian wards. The Australians pushed forward as fast as possible and on that same day obtained the surrender of Benghazi. Dawn came cold and clear.

A department of about thirty Italian medium tanks made one last, gallant but vain attack against the barrier of British armored vehicles; the tankers heroically loaded the British anti-tank guns by overwhelming them and being hit. It was a fierce fight, and the last M13 / 40 was hit by the last British anti-tank gun that remained efficient in front of the command tent of O'Connor: the attempt failed and the infantry surrendered immediately.

'O Connor sent Wavell a short clear message to announce the victory: *Fox killed in the open.*

The 10th Army thus left 101 of its M 13/40 tanks on the field, thirty-nine of which, largely tanks of the XXI Battailon, were intact; only seven thousand Italians and 1,300 Libyans (remains of the Libyan Army Corps and the *Fanti dell'Aria* paratroopers) escaped British captivity. 130,000 soldiers, 400 tanks and 1,200 cannons fell in British hands.

The Australian Official History would say,

After the fighting had ended the desert looked like a film producer's conception of a battlefield. For ten miles the stony floor was littered with hundreds of Lancia and Fiat trucks, many overturned and splintered by shell fire, and with dozens of dark green tanks with crews dead inside them. There were lines of abandoned field guns with ammunition boxes scattered round.

The Italian Air Force also suffered serious losses during the Wavell offensive: 564 aircraft, of which 200 were shot down or destroyed on the ground, the others abandoned during the folding.

The British went as far as Agedabia, and stopped there.

Agedabia, wrote Mario Tobino, is composed of a few houses in the desert, at the beginning of Cyrenaica, in the middle of an expanse. There, Wavell's cunning had ended, the bersaglieri had resisted with his chest, just to resist, and they were dead.

(...) The Agedabia plain on the right, towards the south, rises slightly in a rise. From that, tanks and armored cars of the Nile Division had sprung up.

Agedabia that day swarmed with fugitives, with units without orders, without vehicles; in front there was the immense Sirtica; behind them the enemy advanced calmly and cheerfully.

Some *Bersaglieri*, with rifles, a negligible number of tanks called *matchboxes* as small and fragile as they were, lined up on the plain, while on one side there was the tingling of uncertain, shocked soldiers, without a flag. It was a short fight. The *Bersaglieri* had only youth beyond their chests.

As a cross, they placed two crossed tablets taken from the wooden boxes of Naples' pasta; the *Bersaglieri* still alive, while they were about to be sent prisoners, they wrote the names on them with a pencil.

On the cross each was put his own helmet of *bersagliere*.

The prisoners then went to Egypt lined up in black lines. The field of Agedabia remained with its thin crosses, with those hats on top, the few *matchboxes* overturned and forged; in the sand the teeth of the remaining *Bersaglieri* began to laugh.

GRAZIANI LEAVES, ROMMEL ARRIVES

Marshal Graziani on 8 February sent the following telegram to Mussolini; its text denounces the physical and moral collapse of Marshal, now the ghost of the conqueror of Somalia:

> *Duce*, the latest events have severely depressed my nerves and my strength, so much so as not to allow me to hold the command any longer in the fullness of my faculties. If, for a false feeling of self-love, I kept silent, I would feel greatly guilty. I have tried in every way to make people understand the truth. I have not been listened to. I am sure that a new energy will be able to do much more than I do in the decisive phase of the operations, which are being prepared here.

General Italo Gariboldi was appointed New Governor General of Libya. Before returning to Italy, Graziani set the operational criteria to be followed for the air defense of Tripolitania:

> Object: Operational directives.
> - Etc. Commander 5th Army
> - Etc. Commander of the 5a *Squadra Aerea*
> - Mr. General Intendant
> - Mr. Superior Commander of the Engineers Corps
>
> I summarize and precise the directives to which our action must be informed to counter the eventual westward enemy advance:
>
> - Function of the Homs – Kussabat barrage in the act of constitution with the troops that flowed from Cyrenaica.
> Stop the enemy advance both towards Tripoli and towards Tarhuna.
> - Task of the *Ariete* Armored Division: to be ready to maneuver on the side of the enemy should he abandon the Homs – Kussabat barrier.
> - Sirte garrison function: maintain contact with the enemy and keep him as long as possible, delaying his march by any means. If pressed by overwhelming forces, disengage by opposing subsequent resistance to a knight of the coast.
> Available forces: all those present today in Sirte, including the entire 2nd *Celere* Artillery.
> - Therefore concentrate immediately on Tarhuna, together with some anti-tank weapons that the commander of the 5th Army will deem possible to remove from the sectors of coverage (Tripoli - Zuara).
> - Task of the entrenched camp in Tripoli: to put in the maximum possible efficiency, to increase the accommodation capacity of the port and to study the constitution of some mobile columns, with only fire means, for possible maneuvers outside the entrenched camp.
> Aviation task: of vital importance in these phases: keep the enemy's movements on the coast under constant control and delay any advance by any means.

The Italian Marshal then ordered to put the entrenched field of Tripoli in maximum efficiency, both for possible enemy offenses and, above all, to increase the port's disembarkation capacity for the reinforcements that had to (and should have arrived weeks before) arrive from 'Italy.

On 11 February Graziani was already returning in Rome.

During exactly two months the British, Indian and Australian troops, no more than two Divisions with a total force of 31,000 men, had made an advance for 800 kilometers destroyed an Italian army of ten Divisions, captured about 130,000 prisoners plus 850 guns, 400 wagons and thousands of trucks and various vehicles. British casualties were overall less than 2,000 men: 500 dead, 1,373 wounded and 55 missing.

But the British now had only 40 MK VI / B light tanks, some *Rolls Royce* 1924 and 5 A9-A10 armored cars and the tanks captured to the Italians; the 20/55mm and 47/32mm captured guns were also used. All the *Matilda* had been destroyed. The British troops had also lost all connection to the rear.

A famous study on Beda Fomm, by Kenneth Macsey, defines this battle, taking the words of Wavell, *The Classic Victory*: but it would have been more accurate to call it a *Pyrrhic victory*, as seen less than a month later.

On February 5, the first day of the battle of Beda Fomm, Hitler had written to Mussolini to express his concern for the campaign in North Africa as a whole, offering the help of a full armored Division, provided that the Italians they held on and did not fall back on Tripoli. Five days later Mussolini accepted the offer.

On 11 February *General der Panzertuppe* Erwin Rommel arrived in Rome to receive the assurance that the first line of defense in Tripolitania would have been on Sirte. Three days later a German reconnaissance battalion and an anti-tank battalion of the *5. Leiche-Division* reached Libya, while on January 25 the 132nd *Ariete* Armored Division had started landing in Tripoli.

O'Connor was ordered to return to Cairo to assume the role of Commander in chief of British troops in Egypt and at the insistence of the War Cabinet and the Chiefs of Staff a thin veil of cover troops was left to defend the immense conquered territory.

It was the end of Italy's parallel war.

What had happened in Cyrenaica was stigmatized without too many words by Mussolini in a speech to the Tuscan Leaders of Fascist National Party:

> Because the Italian people suffered in the first retreat from Cyrenaica very rightly, because they fought little, because there was a surprise, because there were too many prisoners: one hundred and twenty thousand.

And the *Duce* was even clearer, a month later, about Graziani:

> I am perfectly convinced that if Italo Balbo had been in command of the troops operating in Libya in December 1940, we would not have had the failure that we had to deplore. He would have disengaged himself. However, he would not have remained four hundred kilometers away from the line of fire, a costume which I will never deplore enough and which has led to unpleasant comparisons between the German generals and some of our generals [means Rommel and Graziani, who remained in Cyrene in a grave Roman, editor's note]. This is my belief. Conviction due to the knowledge of very precise facts that took place afterwards.

The defeat at Sidi el Barrani and the following events constitute the worst defeat in Italian military history, proportionally worse even than the defeat suffered at Caporetto on 24 October 1917. But, was as after Caporetto, the war was not still over.

Ariete Division's tanks in Tripoli's Harbour, January 1941
(Drawing by Kurt Caesar. Author's collection.)

CONCLUSIONS.

After entering the Italian war, the forces present in Libya had to face the French and British threats: in Cyrenaica, British troops had occupied some Italian garrisons on the border with Egypt. The situation improved considerably when France asked for the armistice to Germany, and later to Italy. French troops in Tunisia were dismissed.

It was the end of June 1940: the Governor of Libya was the Air Marshal Italo Balbo. Following an unfortunate aviation accident, Balbo perished, hit by friendly fire in the Tobruk sky on June 28th. In his place, Marshal of Italy Rodolfo Graziani, Chief of Staff of the Army, internationally renowned military and colonialist expert, was placed at the head of the Libyan colony. As soon as he arrived in the government building in Tripoli he found the order addressed to the late Balbo, to attack Egypt by the 15th of July, Graziani. who had not had the opportunity before the departure to speak with Badoglio and Mussolini, from that moment began the exchange of telegrams, letters, and jokes between Graziani, Badoglio, and the Duce, which lasted for months until the fateful and categorical order of attack imparted by Mussolini exclusively for political reasons, in view of the German invasion of the British Isles given for imminent from Berlin.

Graziani was against an advance in the Libyan desert without adequate preparation: the war in the desert was not a traditional war fought in European territory, but involved enormous logistical efforts. The Italian Divisions were poorly equipped, did not have sufficient anti-tank and anti-aircraft weapons and were troops with little mobility, since they had few vehicles, and as Graziani knew well from the time of the conquest of Cufra and the Ethiopian countryside, mobility was in the desert basic.

The troops, on foot, were hopeless: and the number of men, in this case, was a weight and not an advantage. In the months preceding the offensive, Graziani, failing to obtain results, tried to climb over the hierarchical ladder by directly addressing the Duce himself and Galeazzo Ciano; at the beginning of September Mussolini, unnerved by the pressing requests for reinforcements from the Italian Marshal, assumed all responsibility for the company. Graziani obeyed and invaded Egypt. Sufficient reinforcements had not arrived from Italy in efficient weapons, artillery, vehicles and tanks, so Graziani did everything possible to remedy the logistical problem, transporting all the artillery of the 5th Army. located on the Tunisian border at the 10th deployed in Cyrenaica). So also for tanks. The tank battalions consisted of three-ton light tanks, armed only with machine guns with little autonomy; the medium tanks were at height, the M13 / 40, which arrived later were the best on the African front, but used not in mass in adequate formations but only as support to the infantry in small groups.

The rapid war of the Italians in Spain, which had guaranteed so many successes in Malaga, Biscay, and especially in Aragon and Catalonia, seemed to have been simply forgotten, despite the presence of Berti, who had also commanded the Volunteer Troop Corps, and from Bergonzoli.

What makes it even more incredible is that the real creator of the *guerra di rapido corso*, rapid-going war was Marshal Rodolfo Graziani, true proponent of the mechanization of military operations in the desert environment, with the reconquest of Cufra, and, above all, with the campaign of the south front during the Italo-Ethiopian conflict of 1935-1936, in which Bergonzoli and Maletti played an important role as motorized column commanders. It is therefore worth summing up the operations on the Somali front, where the distances, in the Ogaden desert, were hundreds of kilometers.

In the battle of Ganale Doria in January 1936 Graziani divided his troops into three groups, under the command of generals Maletti, Frusci and Bergonzoli, forming three columns.

The center one, commanded by General A. Bergonzoli, was almost totally truck-mounted, with fast tanks, armored cars and machine guns mounted on trucks of the Lancers of Aosta.

On 19 January the fast groups *Aosta* and *Genova* entered Neghelli, the target of the offensive, 380 km away from the starting bases.

Finally in April, while Badoglio was pursuing the defeated Haile Selassie, on the Somali front Graziani on the 14th of the month began the offensive on Harar, five hundred kilometers away.

Graziani's troops, fully motorized, consisted of 38,000 men, of whom 15600 Italians. The first column, under the command of General Nasi, was the strongest and also included the swift grouping commanded by the Consul General of the M.V.S.N. Francesco Navarra Viggiani; it was intended to attack the left side of ras Nasibù, perched on modern defensive lines, which had been designed by Wehib Pasha, one of the defenders of Gallipoli in 1915: the one who had nailed, and eventually forced to re-embark French, English and Australians with their own fortifications, saving - at least temporarily - Constantinople and the Ottoman Empire, and who had known the Italians since the Libyan war.

Nasibù had forces equal in number to those of Italy, moreover well armed with anti-tank guns and machine guns.

The center column (gen. Luigi Frusci) was formed by the 221st Black Shirts Legion of Consul Parini, by seven colonial battalions, two fast-tanks companies and two gang groups and had Dagabur as its objective; the right column (Lieutenant General of the *Milizia Forestale* Augusto Agostini) formed by Carabinieri, *Guardie di Finanza*, Black Shirts and Artillery would have attacked the opposing right.

General Graziani then kept a motorized reserve available.

The Ethiopian troops advanced on Badu Danan, but Graziani did not go to engage them, continuing the push towards Dagabur, penetrating forward thanks to the higher speed, placing themselves behind the entire Nasibu line.

The columns of Frusci and Agostini converged on Dagabur, and at this point, combining the opposite movements of Nasibu and Wehib towards the south and Graziani towards the north, the Italian command realized that it could cut out all the central part and part of the left wing of the entire army of ras Nasibu.

The clashes were so severe that an additional column was formed under the command of General Vernet.

Between 15 and 18 April Nasibu's troops clashed with Libya in Gianagabo. The clashes were fierce: the Libyans enveloped the Ethiopians, and lost about a thousand men, the Ethiopians two thousand. This time the parts were reversed, and it was the Libyan ascari who mutilated the corpses of the Abyssinians.

The Ras Nasibu's units defeated, dispersed in the savannah, porsued by the Libyans troops; others, more fortunate, helped by the arrival of the violent monsoon rains, which procured water, fled to the heights of Chercher, west of Harar.

From April 14 to 30, the Frusci column participated in the battle of the Ogaden along the Gorrahei-Gabredarre-Sassanabeh-Dagabur route, with an advance of 216 kilometers.

The Frusci column was heavily engaged on April 24, and the 221st Legion had the baptism of fire in Hamanlei, which was conquered in the evening.

The Agostini column, to the right of the Frusci column, advanced along the Gherlogubi- Afdub- Uarder- Ado- Curati- Bullaleh- Dagabur route for 260 kilometers.

On April 24 the column attacked the fortified lines of Gunu Gadu, created by Wehib Pasha, one of the defenders of Gallipoli in 1915; the *Milizia Forestale,* the *Dubat-* somali light troops- and *Carabinieri* stood out in particular, flanked by CV33 in a flamethrower version.

On May 5, hindered only by the very heavy rains, the truck-mounted columns took Giggiga, and finally the eight Graziani took Harar where, as announced by a telegram from the *Duce*, Marshal's staff was waiting for him.

Furthermore, in 1939 the maneuvers of the Army of the Po were held, commanded by Graziani himself, who had seen the use on the field of the first Italian armored Divisions, the 131st *Centauro* and the 132nd *Ariete*, and sanctioned the obsolescence of the CV33 and 35 tankettes, but the armored Divisions remained in Italy, first lined up on the French border, then on the Yugoslav one.

As US Major Howard R. Christie writes in his study on the 10th Army, made as thesis for the Master of Military Art and Science at the U.S. Army Command and General Staff College of Fort Leavenwhort,

> Fascist Italy had decided on a new operational doctrine, utilized and tested in the army maneuvers of 1939, which was meant to achieve their strategic goals. This new doctrine of the War of Rapid Decision 24 gave mechanization and the armored forces the pivotal role on the future battlefield. Italy was prepared to fight her enemies with these new forces in northern Italy and to a lesser extent in her colonial possessions. First priority of forces went to the theater of operation that posed the greatest threat to the Italian Empire. In the eighteen months before Italy's entry into World War II, Italy tried to implement the doctrine of the War of Rapid Decision.
> Italy, a noncombatant during the fall of 1939 and the spring of 1940 was intellectually better prepared than most countries that entered World War II.
> This was based on the newly developed doctrine that had evolved in the course of the 1930s and her combat experiences.
> Fascist Italy had the resources and material to attain one strategic goal if it committed its main effort to achieving this goal. An area in which they had a tremendous amount of power and the ability to influence this was in the colony of Italian Libya in North Africa[10].

Despite this, Graziani advanced on Egyptian territory and conquered Sidi el Barrani, a town about a hundred kilometers from Bardia. The British tried to thwart the Italian advance only with their rearguards and retreated to the entrenched camp of Marsa Matruh.

---

[10] H. R. Christie, *Fallen Eagles: the Italian 10th Army in the opening campaign in the western desert, June 1940 - December 1940*, U.S. Army Command and General Staff College, Fort Leavenworth 1999, p. 25.

The occupation of Sidi el Barrani was a mistake from both a tactical and strategic point of view: the losses inflicted on the British were insignificant, the supply lines of the Royal Army extended into hostile and inhospitable territory; it was immediately clear how impossible it was to continue the advance on Marsa Matruh. Reached the goal, Graziani hastened to communicate to the Supreme Command that the occupation of Sidi el Barrani was at the time, the maximum limit of the Italian invasion, and that at the time Marsa Matruh was to be considered unreachable without adequate reinforcements. In the autumn of 1940 the Italian troops built a bituminous road and an aqueduct from Bardia – Sollum to Sidi el Barrani in record time, works that became necessary, because during the rearguard fighting, the British had polluted the wells and destroyed the only existing road. The tactical situation was in favor of the British, the Italian troops were not mobile and had placed themselves in defense in the desert, in an unfavorable territory.

In addition, Italian anti-tank weapons were very scarce and, moreover, out of date. Graziani, understanding the delicate situation of the troops, knowing the numerous enemy forces, tried several times to ask for vehicles and armored vehicles to Italy to be able to face the enemy in battle, but the invasion of Greece on October 28, 1940 meant that utte Italian resources were destined for this campaign. Italian industrial resources were made available to the Greek campaign, which immediately revealed the need for men and materials. In Libya the situation was undoubtedly very serious. Graziani proposed to Badoglio and Mussolini to create an armored force in Libya, even if scarce in number, that could maneuver with satisfactory results against the enemy, who was equipped with over 400 medium and light tanks.

The German *Oberkommando*, observing the objective Italian difficulties in North Africa, thought of helping the shaked ally by proposing the sending of specialized troops. Hitler made this proposal to the *Duce* during the Brenner meeting on October 4, 1940; refusing the Germanic aid of armored vehicles that was offered to Italy by the Führer on that occasion was a very serious mistake. But Mussolini did not want German aid, which would put an end to the parallel war that the *Duce* intended to fight without interference from Germany. Libya was thus practically abandoned to itself, and in December 1940- February 1941 the Italian troops were crushed by the opposing technical and doctrinaire superiority during the operation *Compass* .

In the area between Sollum and Sidi el Barrani, Graziani had few footed binary Divisions, corresponding to British brigades and anti-tank vehicles practically non-existent; while the British forces had an Armored Division reinforced by many mobile regiments, equipped with modern artillery and armored personnel carriers, to which with the reinforcements would have been added selected units such as the 6th *Australian Division*. The 10th Army was seriously deficient: it dispersed its conspicuous forces in defense of the positions conquered at Sidi Barrani, in entrenched positions, very separate and not tactically connected to each other; in the absence of armored reserves, this provision exposed Italian troops to the risk of being circumvented, destroyed in groups, by an undoubtedly more mobile and mechanized enemy.

In truth, Graziani did not fail to repeatedly highlight the shortcomings of the deployment of the 10th Army, without however having the material means to resolve the situation. The position of Sidi el Barrani was to be a temporary position in view of the advance on Marsa Matruh and Alexandria, a place waiting for Italian supplies that could give the decisive boost to the advance in Egypt to the Suez Canal and the Delta.

After months of waiting for supplies to arrive on site, troops were discouraged. The defensive action in the desert carried out by Italian troops without means had little chance of success against a technically superior enemy. The only solution to avoid the disaster that the 10th Army would encounter could be that of a retreat from Sidi el Barrani to the promontory of Sollum, a retreat which was however impossible both for reasons of prestige and because the Italian Divisions that had implemented a retreat to feet would have been hit by enemy armored forces. If Graziani's troops had had the trucks and tanks in Sidi-el-Barrani they would not have used these means for folding, but for the for the offensive with objective Alexandria.

The reason of the Italian defeat at Sidi el Barrani is therefore to be found in the Italian invasion of Egypt in September 1940, added to the lack of supplies given by the Motherland to the 10th Army.

If the Duce had not given the order to attack Egypt, for political reasons, Graziani without having received the reinforcements he asked for, would never have moved from the Cyrenaic border.

Operation E was conducted, as had happened with Greece, with improvisation and total underestimation of the enemy. It was a defeat that did not turn into a catastrophic disaster, thanks to the help, even if accepted too late, by Hitler's Germany, which intervened in the second decade of February 1941, initially limited to the *5. Leiche-Division* and the *15.Panzer-Division*- with its own armored forces in Marmarica. The campaign of Sidi el Barrani and the subsequent retreat remain, therefore, only Italian weapons, the tomb seal on the parallel war.

The conquest of Alexandria and the occupation of the Delta would have represented the blockade to British merchant and military traffic and free access to Italian East Africa: a conduct of the war that derived from a colonial vision therefore; but Suez and Alexandria were an impossible goal to achieve without the armored and motorized forces that could break the armed British defense that was waiting for the enemy in Marsa Matruh.

Having to wait three months for supplies, distracted by the emergency of the Greek-Albanian front, did not serve to achieve the goal; the advanced position of Sidi el Barrani, a location without defense in the ground, was overwhelmed by the strong English motorcycle-armored columns. Within two months the Italian 10th Army was completely destroyed, and the Italian military prestige definitively compromised in the eyes of the Allied propaganda.

For Christie the reason for the Italian defeat was above all one: not having followed the doctrine of the *guerra di rapido corso* that the Italians - and Graziani! - had adopted since the campaign against the Ethiopians in Somalia in 1936, developed in Spain and during the maneuvers of the Po Army in 1939, an army whose commander was Marshal Graziani.

If the Italians had applied their tactical doctrine, the British would have been defeated; the main fault of the defeat therefore falls on Graziani, who, in addition to commanding from the rear and attacking Egypt yielding to the pressure of Rome (but could he have opposed Mussolini?) did not use the tactical doctrine that he himself had contributed to give birth to , who knew well and which if used well would lead to success:

None of the problems facing the Italian Army in Libya were insurmountable. The British position in Egypt was precarious at best. All the Italian Army had to do was act and they would have forced the British back to the Nile River or defeated them soundly. The key factor for the Italian Army was in its senior leader. The supreme commander, Marshal Graziani, had utilized and showed a direct understanding of the new form of mechanized warfare in an earlier conflict but failed to employ it in his invasion of Egypt. As leader of the Italian forces he was the one individual that could have chosen to utilize the proper force and doctrine for the Italian army to be successful in its goals. Marshal Graziani had last fought a European enemy in World War One. His rise to general officer and subsequent claims to victory were against Libyans and Ethiopians. He proved to be timid in fighting against an European enemy that had the capability in defeating him versus an enemy that only had the ability in delaying him. This may have inhibited his ability to make bold and aggressive plans. Marshal Graziani's ability to command such a large organization may be the key to his defeat. He commanded from the rear and was not a front line commander. Being in the rear caused delays in receiving information from the forward-deployed units and those in contact. Marshal Graziani would make decisions based on old and inaccurate information. He would also send orders directly to units, bypassing layers of command. This caused great confusion on the battlefield. It violated the principle of war know as Unity of Command. Marshal Graziani failed to implement a plan that would assure success and the plan he did implement, he did not pursue with a sense of urgency or aggressiveness. He had the experience, doctrine and available forces to defeat an enemy whose position was tenuous at best. Ultimately all responsibility for success or failure rests with the commander.

Furthermore, last but not least, Graziani not only had Wavell in front of him - Wawell stayed at the *Shepheard* hotel in Cairo, where he had his headquarters, in hindsight far more distant from the front (and comfortable!) from the Cyrene's Greek tomb used by Graziani and on which there was so much irony, starting from Mussolini himself- but above all an innovative general, stubborn and tenacious like O'Connor, one of the few British officers to have studied and pondered the theories on the use of armored vehicles and on the modern war of Fuller and Liddle Hart, at the head of fewer men, but professional and well trained soldiers, and not of leverage like most of the Italians: when the leverage is introduced also in the United Kingdom there will no longer be such difference, and Italians will be often successful against the British.

In addition, Graziani's temper was no longer, as we said, the one before the 1937 attack on Addis Ababa, and the Marshal was aware of his technical inferiority to the point of coordinating very badly. or not to coordinate the retreat and defense of Cyrenaica at all: ironically with a Gott or a Montgomery the results would have been much more positive, but with O'Connor and his strategic ability this proved to be suicidal. Another neglected aspect is how too many units tended to surrender easily without engaging in combat: as seen was not the case for the Fascist Militia, which was the most tenacious in defending itself, always deliberately neglected by post-war historiography - nor for the units with greater selection, spirit of body and training, tankers, *Bersaglieri* and also the Libyan paratroopers of the *Fanti dell'Aria* Btl.of Lieutenant Colonel Tonini.

The moral factor should not be underestimated: the Italians Command's fault was not having been able to inspire self-confidence in the units during the retreat - which will then succeed in Rommel with excellent results - who instead suffered a real sense of inferiority towards the enemy, considered unstoppable; in this regard, we read in the telegram on operations in Libya sent by Wavell and attached to the document W.P. (41) 32 drawn up by the British War Cabinet on 16 February 1941, recalling how the appearance of British armored vehicles spread insecurity if not real panic among the retreating units, which tended to stop and place themselves on the defensive rather than trying to break through (but in Beda Fomm it had gone differently!):

> In early days units of armoured Division penetrated and temporarily cleared tracts of hostile territory running into thousands of square miles. Gradually they were pressed back by establishment successive defended localities by forces numerically superior as ten to one employing artillery twenty or thirty to one. Result, this extraordinary moral ascendency evident every stage of operations leading to capture Benghazi. If British armoured units even in small number- appeared to threaten line of retreat, first Italian impulse was to hesitate and then assume defensive instead of trying to break through. Using different methods of surprise bold use of numerically inferior forces worked time after time[11].

Latimer writes about this in his *Operation Compass. Wavell's Whirlwind Offensive*, which, beyond the Allied propaganda, the Italians were brave, but what they lacked was collective morale:

> The Italians were far from the cowards protrayed in Allied press (very much a devise from home comsuption) and proved consistently that they did not lack individual courage. Innumerable examples are testament to their individual bravery. What they lacked was collective morale, which, given the deficiences of their military machine was hardly surprising (...)

And yet Wavell stressed the quality of the British material compared to the Italian one, more for reasons related to war supplies than anything else, he would be inclined to think, given the serious wear and tear suffered by British vehicles at the end of Compass reduced to just 40 MK VI / B tanks, in addition to those captured to the Italians:

> For nearly eight months armored Division has been employed without rest. Vehicles which had already withstood strain protracted operations in worst possible conditions sand and heat were able in last dash to make final and protracted burst which completely surprised enemy. Weight for class Italian tanks, many of them newly delivered by manufacturers, proved no match for British products.

How much propaganda there was in such considerations would be proved by the subsequent events with the exploits of the *Armata Corazzata Italo- tedesca* (A.C.I.T.), or *Panzerarmee Afrika*, which would have reduced the Wavell's bragging of 1941 as had happened with the Italian ones in the summer of 1940.

---

[11] http://filestore.nationalarchives.gov.uk/pdfs/small/cab-66-15-wp-41-32-5.pdf

"Where we can win England, England will be win"
Adolf Hitler, January 30, 1941.
(drawing by Kurt Caesar,
the caption is the original German one).
(author's collection).

CHRONOLOGY

1940

June 10.
The Kingdom of Italy declares war on France and the United Kingdom.

June 11th.
First Italian air attack on Malta.

June 24.
Armistice between Italy and France at Villa Incisa in Olgiata (Rome). Dismantling of the Mareth line.

June 28.
Italo Balbo's shot down in Tobruk. He is replaced by Rodolfo Graziani.

July 9.
Naval battle of Punta Stilo.

August 3.
The Italians invade British Somalia.

August 19.
the British abandon British Somalia.

September 13.
The Italian invasion of Egypt begins (*Operation* E); conquest of Sollum.

September 16.
Occupation of Sidi el Barrani.

September 17th.
After the defeat in the Battle of England, the *Seelöwe* operation was abandoned.

October 4.
Meeting between Mussolini and Hitler at the Brenner Pass. Mussolini declines the offer of German troops for northern Africa.

October 28.
Italy invades Greece.

11-12 November.
British air raid on Taranto *(Operation Judgment)*. Slightly damaged the battleships *Littorio* and *Caio Duilio*, seriously the *Cavour*.

December 9.
Start of *Operation Compass*. General Piero Maletti falls in combat.

December 10.
Fall of Sidi el Barrani.

December 11th.
The 7th Armored Division captures Buq Buq.

December 17.
The British reconquer Sollum.

December 24.
The 6th Australian Division invests the stronghold of Bardia.

1941

3-5 January.
Battle of Bardia.

January 21-22
Australians besiege and capture Tobruk.

January 23.
The Sabratha Division and the Air Infantrymen block the 6th Australian Division in Derna.

January 24.
Battle of el Mechili.
On the same day, the first units of the 132nd Armored Division *Ariete* landed in Tripoli.

January 28.
The Italians disengage from the Derna line; the 10th Army begins folding down via Balbia.

February 5.
The 7th Arm. Division places road blocks on via Balbia near Beda Fomm.

February 6.
British occupation of Benghazi.

6- 7 February.
Battle of Beda Fomm.
General Tellera falls in combat; surrender of the remains of the 10th Army.

February 8.
Graziani asks to be repatriated; Italo Gariboldi replaces him.

February 10.
Mussolini accepts German aid to Libya.

February 11th.
Graziani returns to Italy; Generallutnant Erwin Rommel arrives in Rome.

February 12.
Rommel arrives in Tripoli.

February 14.
The first German units of the *Deutsches Afrika Korps* arrive in Tripoli.

The German *Deutsche Afrika Korps* are coming.

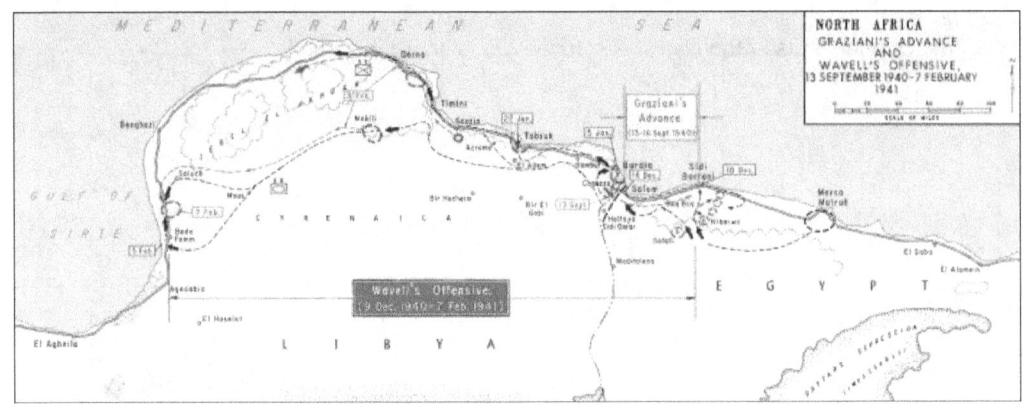

The North African Theatre, 1940-1941.

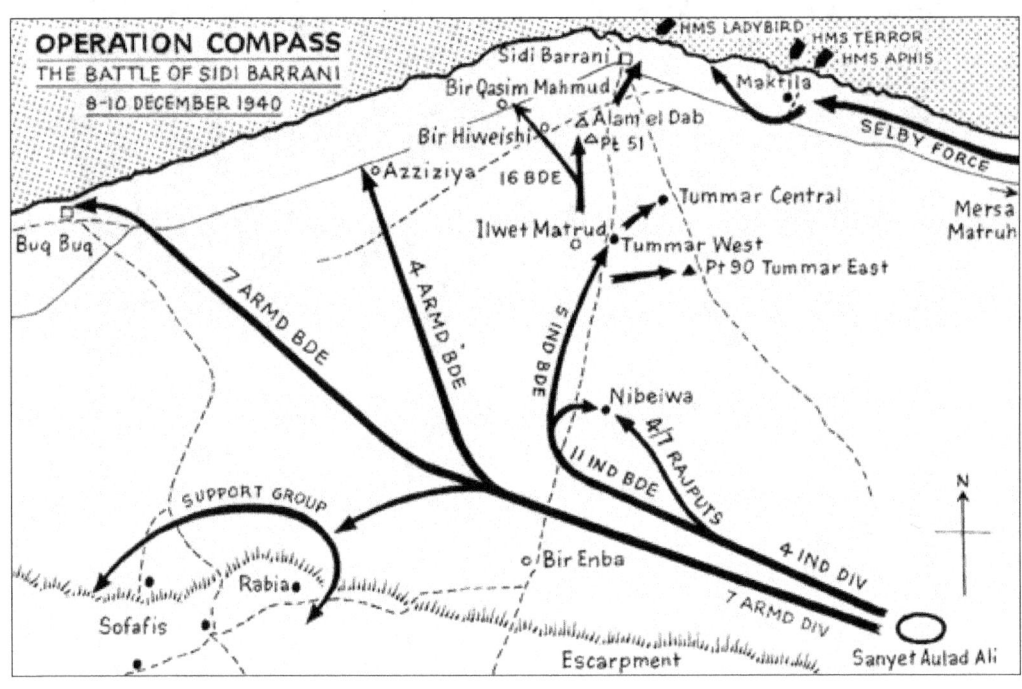

Operation *Compass*. The battle of Sidi el Barrani, 8-10 December 1940.

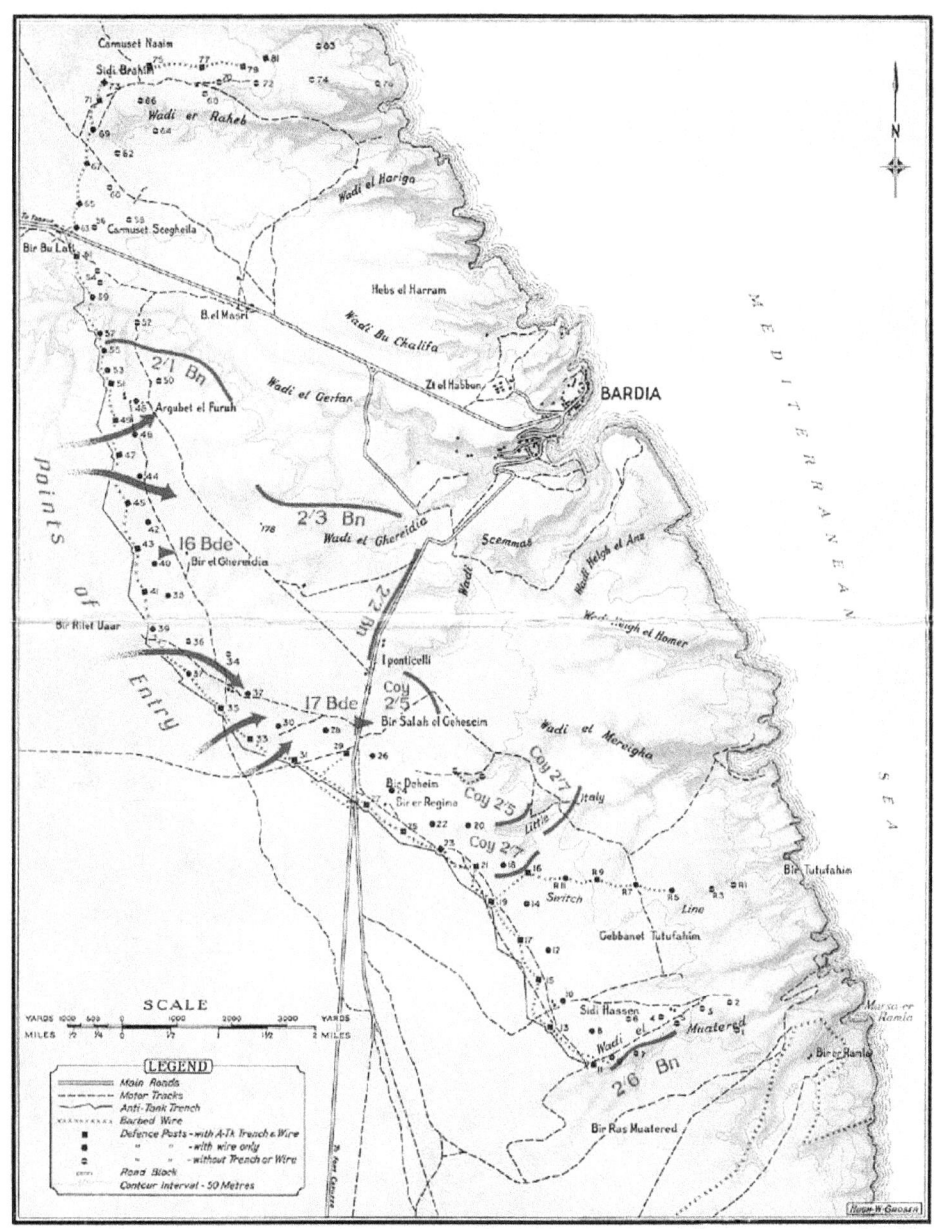

Bardia, January 3, 1941.

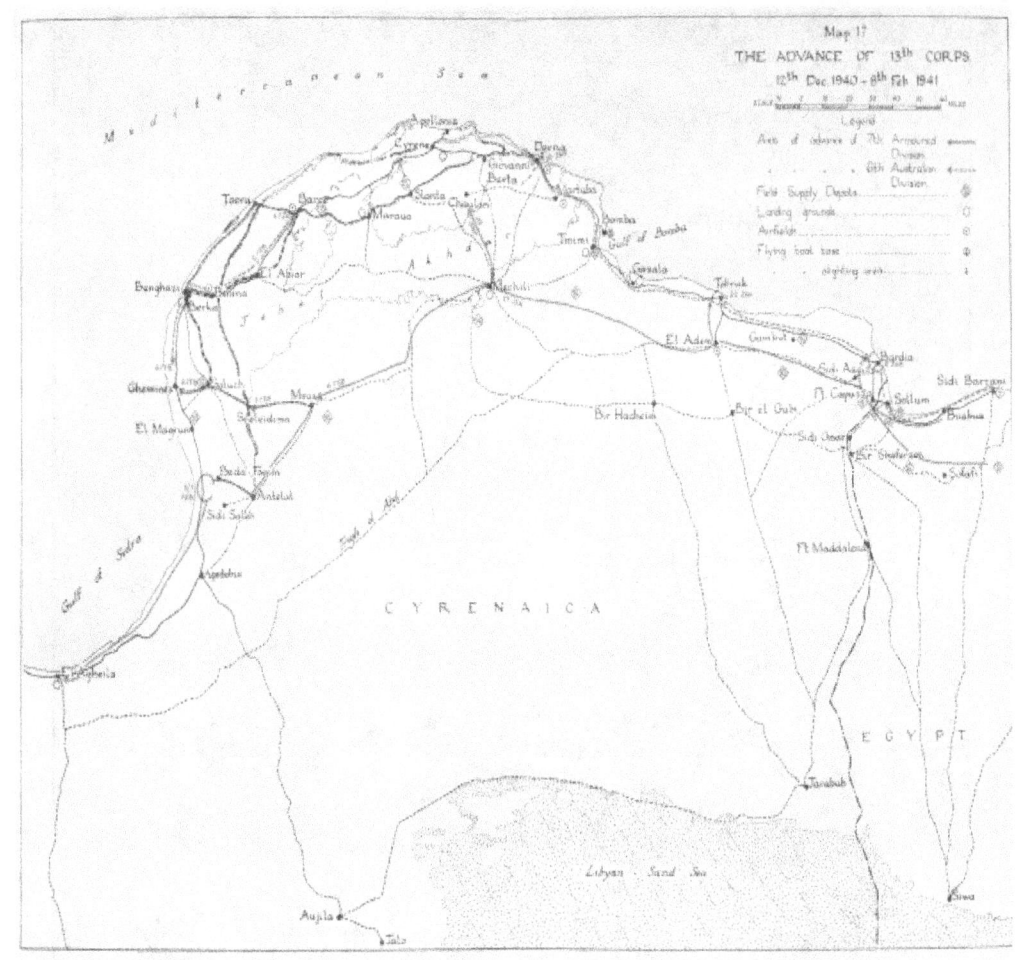

The invasion of Cyrenaica.

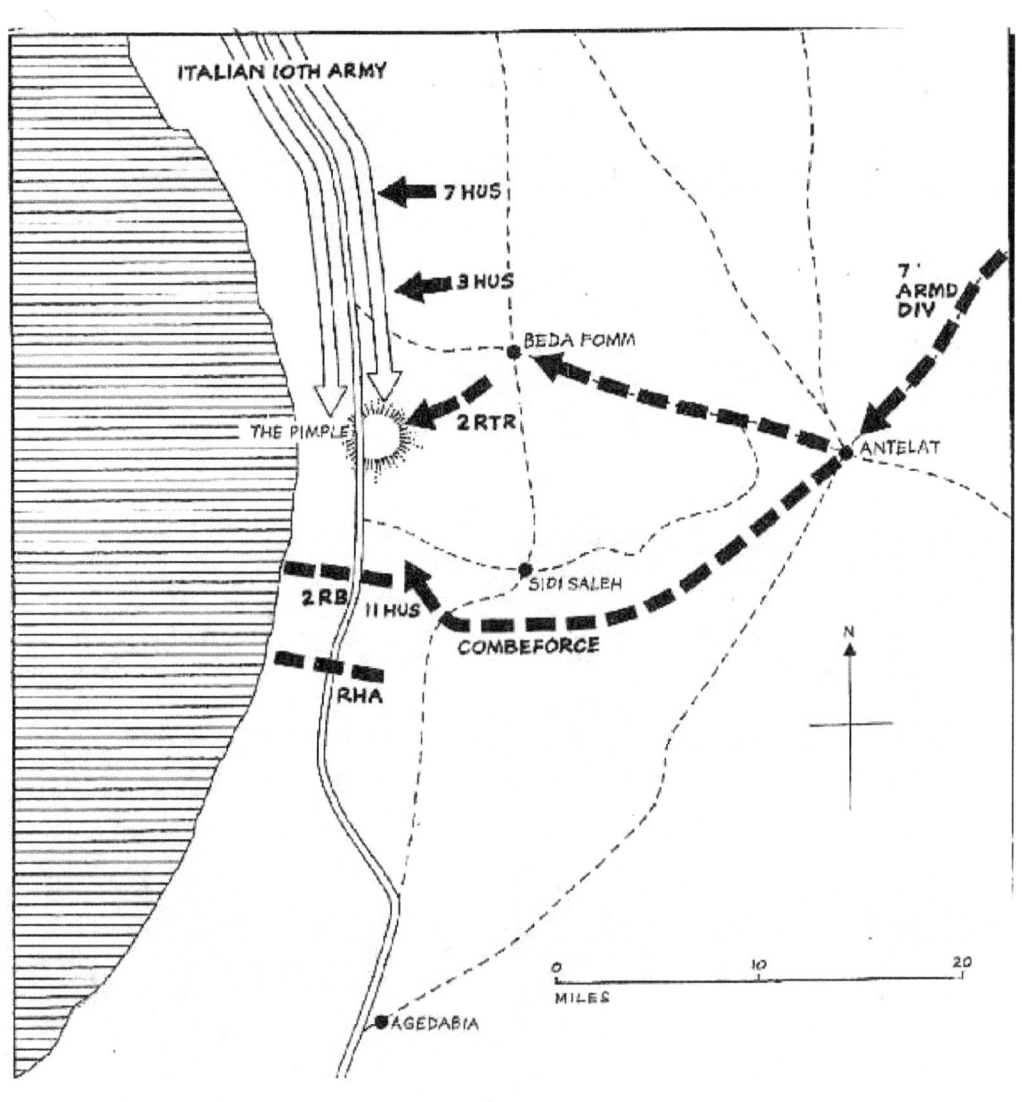

Battle of Beda Fomm, 5-7 February 1941.

Air Marshal Italo Balbo, Governor of Libya. Against the war and the alliance with Germany, he fell victim to "friendly fire" on Tobruk at the start of the war.

June 1940 The Air Marshal Italo Balbo inspects a *Morris CS9* armored car he himself captured.

Libyan paratroopers of the *Fanti dell'Aria* Btl at Castel Benito, 1940.

July 1, 1940. Transfer of the bodies of Balbo and the other fallen from Tobruk to Tripoli

Tripoli, 3 July 1940. Italo Balbo's funeral; the Air Marshal was shot down in Tobruk on 28 June.

The coffin of the Air Marshal Italo Balbo

Libyan Ascari of the P.A.I. (Italian Africa's Police)

Black Shirts defiling in Tripoli at *Passo romano* (goose step)

Marshal of Italy Rodolfo Graziani who replaced Italo Balbo after his death.

Annibale Bergonzoli (1 November 1884 – 31 July 1973), nicknamed *barba elettrica"*, "Electric Whiskers", fought in World War I, the Italo-Ethiopian War, the Spanish Civil War and World War II. In 1940 He commanded the defences of Bardiaa. In February 1941, after the disastrous Battle of Beda Fomm, Bergonzoli surrendered to Australian forces.

An Italian sentry scans the horizon with binoculars from an elevated position in the desert, September 1940

Sir Archibald Wavell in Field Marshal's uniform.

General Richard O'Connor.

Italian soldiers in the *Jebel*, summer 1940

Savoia Marchetti SM 79 *Sparviero* on an airfield in Libya, August 1940

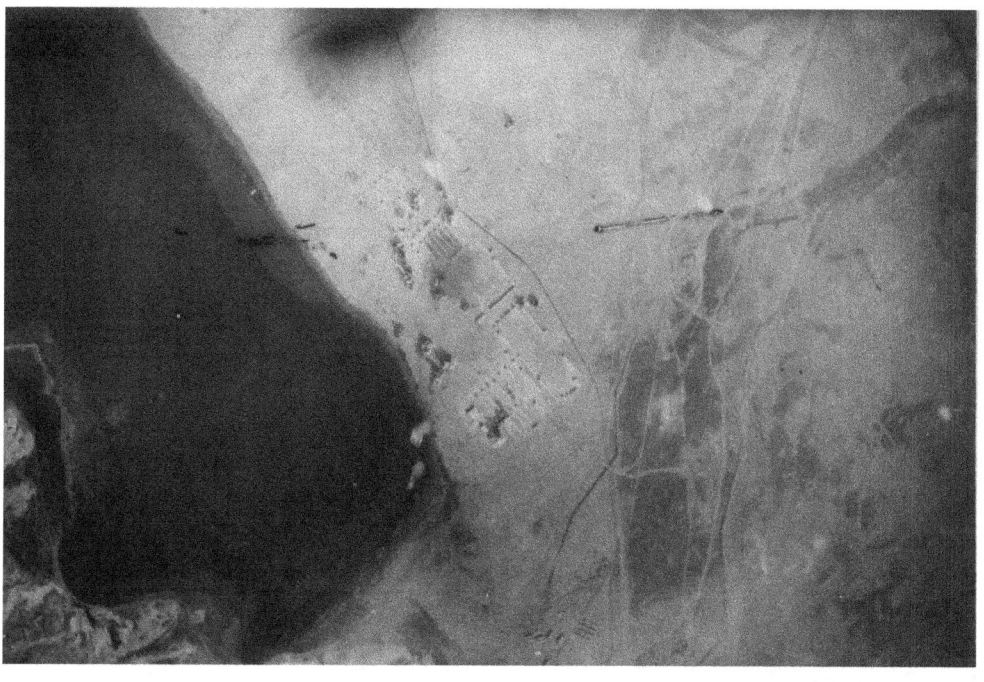

Italian bombing of British positions during the Graziani offensive, September 1940.

Damnaged SM79 in an Libyan airfield, sumer1940

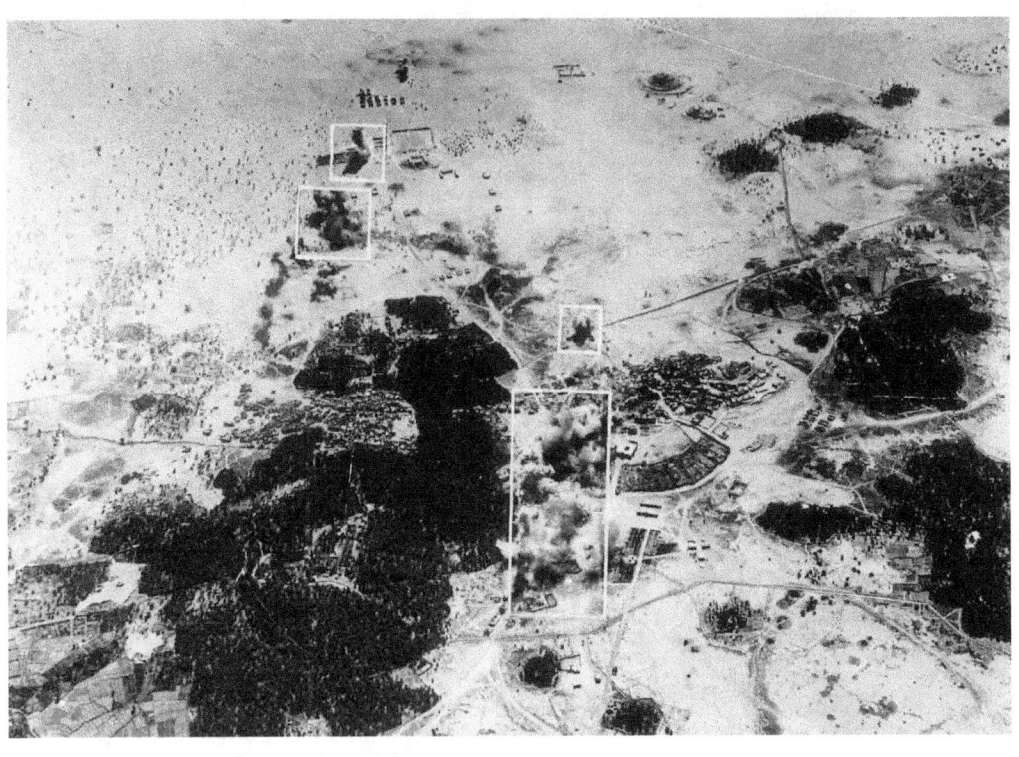

Italian bombing of the Siwa oasis in Egypt

Savoia Marchetti SM79 bomber, August 1940

Shooting of a Bristol Blenheim by the Italian fighters in a photo retouched for propaganda

Airfield in North Africa. Note the Fiat G50 *Freccia* and Fiat CR 42 *Falco* fighters'

Italian airmen with ammunition for SM79 machine guns

The bay of Sollum on the Libyan-Egyptian border

Black Shirts advancing. Note the two Fiat 34 MG.

Black Shirts of the 2nd *28 Ottobre* Division, 1940.

Trucks AS37 of the Maletti Group marching towards Sidi el Barrani

A British officer take prisoner

Black shirts of *3 Gennaio* Division on an armed truck in the Egyptian desert in September 1940

CV 33 tankettes advancing. In the foreground a command tank, recognizable by the radio antenna.

CV35 flametrower near Sollum, 1940.

Black Shirts assigned to a 47/32 gun in Sidi el Barrani.

Black Shirts of the *3 Gennaio* Division with a 47/32 anti-tank gun in September 1940.

An Italian truck in the desert south of Sidi el Barrani.

M 11/39 Medium tanks at Sidi el Barrani.

M11/39 tanks in the Western Deserts

M 11-39 in combat at Sidi el Barrani

M 11/39 tanks advancing in the Western desert.

Italian 90/53 guns in battery.

Italian vehicles during the advance across the Egyptian border

Distribution of water to the Black Shirts, September 1940

Libyan *Zaptiè* in Sawani el Khur, 1940.
The Zaptiè were the Libyan components of the *Carabinieri* military Police. Note the metal stars (*stellette*) on the collar-patches, brought after the granting of Italian citizenship to the Libyans in 1939.

An artilleryman consumes his ration in the desert

Bersaglieri at rest in decidedly unregulated clothing

Bersaglieri motorcyclists, September 1940

Bersaglieri motorcyclists in the Cyrenaic Jebel

Bersaglieri motorcyclists with Moto Guzzi 500 Alce

Two *Bersaglieri* now become veterans

The arid rocky plateau of Cyrenaic Jebel (for the Italians *Gebel*), the theatre of the battles fought between 1941 and 1943

Black Shirts of the *3 Gennaio* Division to an acoustic detection instrument to detect enemy planes in the Libyan desert in September 1940

Italian Light Artillery in the Western desert, 1940

Black Shirts of the *3 Gennaio* Division resting during the advance on Sidi el Barran

Armoured Trucks of the *3 Gennaio* Division advancing on Sidi el Barrani

An Artilleryman in an Anti-aircraft position , Tripolitania, 1940

90mm Italian anti-aircraft gun, autumn 1940.

The crew of an M13/40 *Centro Radio*

Italian vehicles in the desert

Anti-aircraft mounted guns at Sidi el Barrani

75-27 mod.1911 anti-tank gun

Two officers of the Regia Aeronautica during the construction of an advanced airfield in the Egyptian desert, September 1940.

Black Shierts near Buq Buq

Light tank CV 33, 1940

Italian Artillery gun in position, summer 1940

Sollum destoied

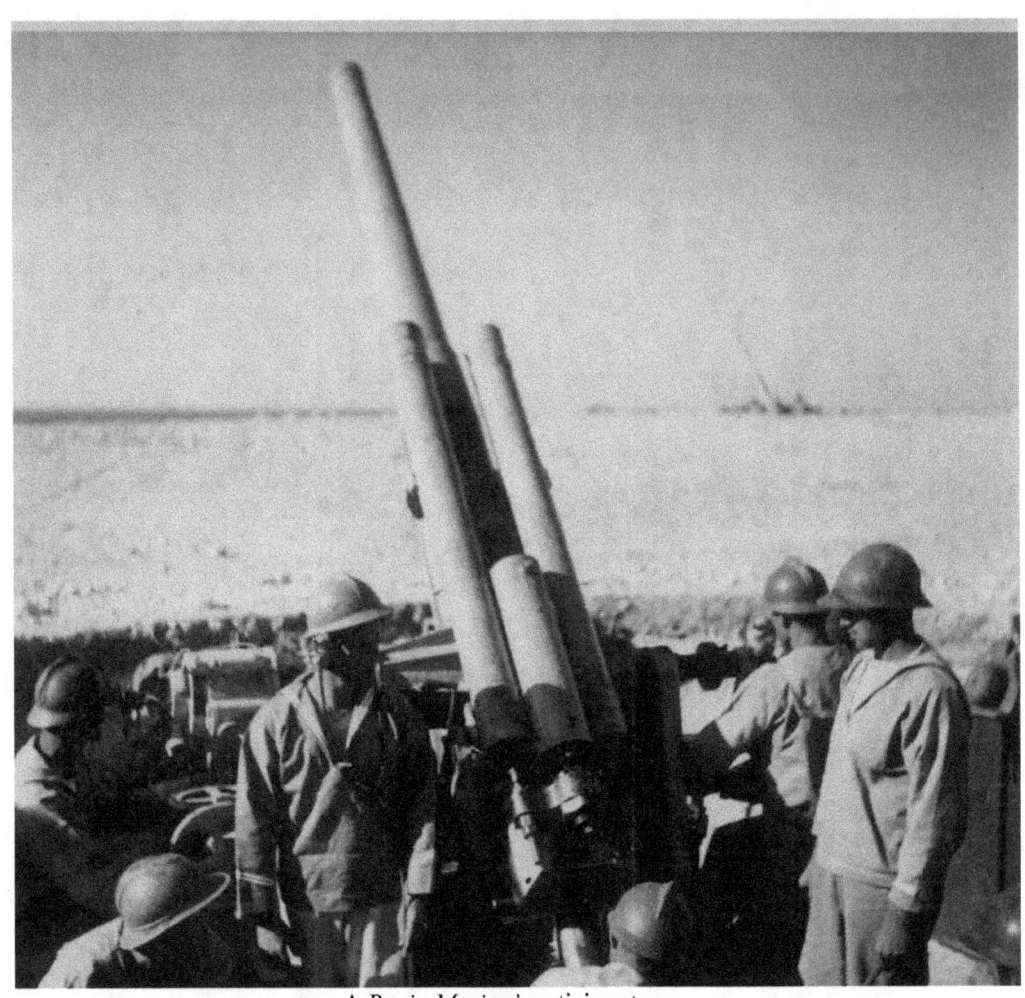
A *Regia Marina's* antiaircrat gun

Cruiser Tank Mk I, Egypt

7th *Royal Tank Regiment* 's Matilda, 19 december 1940

A *Bren Carrier* near a milestone with a *Fascio* along the military road built in Sidi el Barrani by the Italians

Matilda MK II's crew with a captured Italian flag

Italian prisoners taken by the British in Bardia.

British Mk VI in the Western desert, 1940

Two British tankers of the 7th Armored in a break reading an Italian newspaper.

Aa 5-*Pounder* Mark II gun belonging to 1st *Battery*, A *Troop*, *Australian* 21st Field *Artillery Regiment* bombing Bardia, 29 December 1940.

January 3, 1941. Australian troops advancing towards Bardia.

Australian *Bren carrier* in action, 7 January 1941.

Black Shirts captured by the British troops in Bardia, January 1941.

The Cruiser *San Giorgio* on fire after sinking in the port of Tobruk, 22 January 1941

M11 /39 tanks captured by the Australian Troops.

An Australian tankman paints a Kangaroo on the turret of an M13 / 40 captured in Cyrenaica

A British tankman inspects a captured CV33.

O'Connor and other Senior Officers near two Italian M13 / 40 tanks put out of action in Beda Fomm

The commander of the 23rd Army Corps, Annibale Bergonzoli, captured by the British in Beda Fomm. Bergonzoli had earned the nickname of *Electric Whiskers* in March 1937 in Guadalajara, where he commanded the *Littorio* Division, fighting with the bayonet in the front line against International Brigatists, alongside his volounteers, wiile the Division band played by his order *Giovinezza* and the *Royal March* : the Germans of Brigada *Thaelmann* were totally destroied by Bergonzoli's men.

The arrival of the *Deutsche Afrika Korps* in Tripoli in February 1941 changed the ties of forces in North Africa. It was time for Rommel, the *Wustenfuchs*.

Rommel and Gariboldi in Tripoli ispecting the *5. Leiche Division*.

Cirene stronghold. in the foreground, the wreckage of a CR42 *Falco* destroyed during the British offensive. (Kurt Caesar, 1941. Author's collection)

M 13/40 tanks charging
(drawing By Kurt Caesar, 1941. Author's collection)

THE CONQUEST OF SIDI EL BARRANI.
MARSHAL GRAZIANI'S RELATION
TO *COMANDO SUPREMO*, 18 SEPTEMBER 1940.

On September 18, 1940, the Italian Marshal Rodolfo Graziani sent the report on the advance on Sidi el Barrani to the Supreme Command:

The original design of operations essentially involved an attack bypassing the right to be integrated at the appropriate time with a double enveloping action on Sidi el Barrani. Since in the meantime the enemy forces situation was accentuating the densification of mechanized elements within external direct range (Bir el Chreigat - Dar el Brug - Bir Dignaish) which should have been followed by our right wing, I decided to radically change the operational design, concentrating all forces on the left and aiming lightly on Sidi el Barrani for coastal route.

In this way, the trumpeted and truly powerful enemy armored forces operating in the desert would have been cut off from their base and forced to fall back on difficult tracks and deprive all resources. I immediately gave orders.

In summary Libyan Divisions group from Bir el Gobi - Gabr Saleh in the first line between Capuzzo and Ghirba.

XXIII Army Corps in second rank behind Libyan Division. With his powerful advanced deployment of medium and small caliber artillery he had to support Libyan attack. Two quick elements in reserve.

Maletti mixed grouping on the right ready to take advantage of the aforementioned external route, Division *23 Marzo*, all self-loaded on the left.

He developed a two-step maneuver.

Before: movement to reach starting positions.

Second: Sollum et Halfaia outlet attack and rapid advance towards Barrani.

Depending on the situation, I reserved the right to decide when to launch fast columns.

First phase movements took place with some difficulty in the harshness of the desert by the Maletti Group also subjected to repeated aerial bombardments.

Believing it impossible to entrust them with the task of acting in isolation by desert route, I moved it further north, to Ghirba, in close contact with the right of 10th Army.

It was also necessary a day of rest for the rearrangement and reconstruction of logistic equipment. Advancing in force on Sollum and Halfaia which began on day 13 and continuation towards the East they took by surprise an enemy that awaited our main columns further south. From Sidi Omar to Sceferzen.

By evening September 14 Libyan Divisions overwhelmed enemy resistance, they had reached Tidam el Khedim about 25 kilometers from Sollum.

I judged that the decisive moment had come and I immediately ordered that reserve consisting of fast columns *23 Marzo* and Maletti, bypassing Libyan Divisions, aimed decisively on Barrani. Although movement difficulties given poor track conditions and raging ghibli did not allow Sidi el Barrani to be occupied on the day of the 15th, but only the following day, however the maneuver can be considered perfectly successful.

In fact, as soon as it became aware of the threat on Barrani, the English armored Division rushed to fall precipitously along desert tracks, pursued relentlessly, bombed and strafed by our tireless flocks, which sowed destruction and disorder in its ranks.

Most of his vehicles have remained abandoned along the slopes.

Many symptoms have revealed crises, especially petrol and water supplies, as well as disorientation and nervousness in enemy commands.

Behavior, value and spirit of sacrifice all land and air armed forces was superior to all praise, especially bearing in mind ground conditions, a season considered prohibitive by the enemy especially raging suffocating *ghibli* during a decisive day.

23 Marzo's Black Shirts were the first to reach Barrani.

In perfect spirit communion with the Army and Militia revolution, Libyan units gave superb proof.

In just eight days, they walked about 250 kilometers of desert, fighting and serenely suffering aerial offenses and artillery bombings, thus debunking legends spread by enemy propaganda that the Libyans would not have fought.

Overall operation exceeded all expectations because it managed to create surprise in a theater of operations that this a priori surprise excluded.

From a logistical point of view, miracles have occurred.

The Egyptian press believed that between fifteen and twenty thousand men could pass between the sea and the desert and that the passage of trucks and armored cars was very difficult, especially from August to mid-October.

And he concluded verbatim: such an expedition would therefore have 5 chances of success out of 100, and only in the season from November to March. Ends.

Enemy after having made all possible resistance by contrasting palm to palm, he was finally overwhelmed by the maneuver that gripped him and he precipitously retreated to Marsa Matruh destroying and setting fire to deposits, barracks and burying wells.

It can be calculated that it has lost more than half of the more than half of its armored vehicles, among those hit by aviation and those lost in the desert following a disorderly folding.

Aviation worked tirelessly with opposing bombing actions throwing terror among its ranks and protecting marching columns in the bare desert with cruises from hunting in front of which the strong formations of the enemy Gloster have constantly turned their backs.

Where the English critic already mentioned opted that only a few vehicles would pass, during the action about two thousand of them passed, a clear demonstration of a logistical effort of such power that 70 certainly could not have been conceived and much less realized by the British mentality , who would perhaps have preferred to carry out this advanced method by following the construction of a railway like that of Lord Kitchener of good memory in Sudan.

Equal to the effort of the machines was the resistance of our infantrymen of the black shirts and Libyan troops, who under a heat of 50 ° and in the turbines of the sands, raised by the ardent ghibli, were satisfied with the usual liter of water of Neghelli.

One wonders when the British will begin to understand that they are dealing with the strongest colonial army in the world and when they will finally learn about the value of the Italian soldier. They will learn it as soon as possible.

OPERATION *COMPASS* IN THE BULLETINS OF THE ITALIAN *COMANDO SUPREMO*

BULLETIN No. 187 of 11 December:
At dawn on day 9, British armored Divisions attacked our deployment southeast of Sidi el Barrani, held by Libyan troop formations. These troops valiantly resisted in the first half, but after a few hours they were overwhelmed and retreated to Sidi el Barrani. On 9 and yesterday, fighting of exceptional violence took place between enemy troops and ours. The Black Shirt Division on January 3 and the 1st Libyan Division held up against the attack by inflicting extremely serious losses on the enemy. Fighting continues in the area. In one of them, General Maletti fell at the head of his Libyan battalions. Our air force flew at all times over the battle sky, strafing and bombing the enemy armored formations. On the Greek front, the day passed without particularly significant actions.

BULLETIN No. 188 of 12 December:
(...) In Northern Africa, operations are still ongoing. Even yesterday, fierce fighting took place west of Sidi el Barrani, in the Bugbug area. The losses in vehicles and men inflicted on the enemy are considerable. Ours are sensitive too.

BULLETIN No. 189 of December 13:
At the Cyrenaic border, in the area between Sollum and Sidi el Barrani and in the desert area to the southeast, the battle between our troops fighting with great value and the enemy armored columns continued yesterday. Our fighter and bombing squadrons, despite sandstorms raised by the *ghibli*, flew continuously from sunrise to sunset, bombing and setting fire to enemy units. The total number of enemy aircraft shot down in combat from day 9 rises to eighteen. Since the same day, twelve of our aircraft have not returned.

BULLETIN No. 190 of December 14:
In the Cyrenaean border area, fighting continued throughout the day yesterday and in the afternoon; some counterattacks carried out by our troops have slowed down enemy pressure. Our air formations have flown continuously on the battlefield. Our hunt shot down six Glosters in combat; all our planes have returned, some with dead and wounded on board.

BULLETIN No. 191 of 15 December:
After the evacuation of Sidi el Barrani, yesterday - sixth day of the great battle - Italian and English troops clashed bloody from morning to sunset in the desert area of Forte Capuzzo-Sollum-Bardia. Attacks and counterattacks went on and on. The battlefield is sown with groups of armored cars and enemy tanks that burn. But the pressure from enemy forces has not yet eased. The aviation went a long way, with the admirable spirit of sacrifice that distinguishes it, bombing and fighting continuously. In yesterday's fights eleven aircraft were shot down in flames by our fighters. Further checks raise enemy aircraft shot down the previous day to twelve. Six of our bombers have not re-

turned. The enemy carried out bombing actions against the base of Bardia and that of Tripoli. In the latter city two enemy planes were shot down.

BULLETIN N ° 192 of 16 December:
In Cyrenaica, in the border area, the pressure of enemy forces bombed by our air force continued, which inflicted many losses on the armored formations.

BULLETIN No. 193 of December 17:
The eighth day of battle in the desert area of the Cyrenaic front took place with a determination not less than that of the previous days. Our air force, despite the prohibitive weather, has not slowed down its activity, in competition with the resistance of the troops and with its fighters and bombers formations it has strongly worn down the enemy. On the sea, our torpedo bombers hit a 6,000-ton cruiser that had bombed Bardia with two torpedoes. Five of our planes have not returned.

BULLETIN No. 194 of December 18:
In the Cyrenaean border zone, due to the wear and the losses they suffered, enemy troops slowed down their pressure yesterday - the ninth of the great battle. Our artillery has effectively defeated enemy mechanized units, while our air formations have bombed more distant armored units. The torpedoed enemy cruiser in front of Porto Bardia, referred to in Bulletin No. 193, was seen to capsize and sink. The sinking torpedo bombs were in command of the pilot captain Grossi and the lieutenant pilot Barbani, assisted by the observers of the lieutenant Marazio and Riva. Our aircraft bombed British warships that appeared in front of Porto Bardia. The aviation fighter aircrafts opposed the action of our bombers, who shot down a *Gloster* aircraft. Our hunting formations, escorting the bombers, have engaged in combat with enemy fighters: a Hurricane has been shot down; one of our hunting equipment has not returned. (...) On the day of the 16th 5 British fighters were shot down.

BULLETIN No. 195 of December 19:
In northern Africa, the battle in the Bardia area continues where significant concentrations of enemy mechanized vehicles are reported. Some of these formations that had attempted to approach the city were successfully counter-attacked. Our aerial formations have bombed effectively enemy armoured vehicles.

BULLETIN ° 196 of 20 December:
In the Cyrenaic border area, our artillery successfully countered enemy artillery and mechanized vehicles in the Bardia sector. During strafing and bombing, our aerial formations were assaulted by groups of enemy planes. Our formations reacted by supporting a furious battle: two Hurricane were shot down, one of our hunting equipment did not return. In the night from 18 to 19 Alexandria was bombed.

BULLETIN No. 198 of December 22:
In the Cyrenaic border area, actions by the opposing artillery. One of our naval units bombed enemy motorized groups near the coast; a torpedo boat shot down an enemy torpedo bomb. Our air units carried out an intense bombardment against concentrations of troops and mechanized vehicles; moreover, throughout the night, although hampered

by bad weather, they constantly kept under attack the docks and facilities of an enemy advanced base, where fires were caused. The enemy carried out the bombing of our air base in Tripolitania

BULLETIN No. 199 of December 23:
In the Cyrenaic border area the situation is unchanged. Aerial bombardments of an advanced base of the enemy and attacks against its armored vehicles have been renewed. A torpedo bomb hit and sank an English auxiliary cruiser. The enemy bombed some centers in Libya: one dead and three injured.

BULLETIN No. 200 of December 24:
In the Cyrenaic border area, our artillery battled armored personnel carriers and enemy tanks approached our positions. Our bombers carried out a very successful action against mechanized vehicles and against an enemy advanced base. In air combat, our fighter shot down two Hurricane-type aircraft. One of our aircraft has not returned from a reconnaissance.

BULLETIN No. 201 of December 25:
In the Cyrenaic border area the situation is unchanged. The air units continued their bombing and strafing action against opposing mechanized vehicles. The enemy advanced bases were still subjected to intense bombing; outbreaks and fires were noted at an air base. In Tripolitania the enemy bombed the city and port of Tripoli causing some damage.

BULLETIN No. 202 of December 26:
In the Cyrenaic border area around Bardia, lively actions of the enemy artillery countered by ours. An attack on our place in the desert has been repelled. In the night between 24 and 25 and yesterday, an enemy advanced base was subjected to intense aerial bombing: a warship was hit. Furthermore, mechanized vehicle cores were effectively bombed in southern Cyrenaica

BULLETIN No. 203 of December 27:
In the Cyrenaic border area, actions by the opposing artillery and patrols continue. Intense activity of our aviation: bombings were carried out against ships, in the bay of an advanced base, against batteries and against mechanized vehicles. The fighter engaged combat with a large formation of *Gloster*: three enemy aircraft were shot down. One of our aircraft has not returned. In the waters of Cyrenaica, on the morning of the 26th, a maritime reconnaissance hydro sighted and effectively bombed an opponent submarine.

BULLETIN No. 204 of December 28:
In the Cyrenaic border area, on the Bardia front, artillery shots. In an action combined with aviation one of our swift columns destroyed an enemy armoured patrol, capturing its crews. A naval unit carried out an artillery action against the armored units along the coast, dispersing opposing cores and silencing self-propelling artillery. Our bombers continued to hold under their effective offense, yesterday and the previous night, advanced bases and enemy mechanized vehicles. Our fighters sustained lively fights with the opposing one.

BULLETIN No. 205 of December 29:
In the Cyrenaean border area, increased artillery and patrols activities on the Bardia front; action of our swift columns, in cooperation with the air force, which, in the desert region, destroyed some enemy armored cars. Two of our torpedo bombers attacked and hit a monitor and a destroyer. One of our fighter aircraft has not returned.

BULLETIN No. 206 of December 30:
In the Cyrenaic border area, artillery actions continue around Bardia; some small mechanized English units that tried to approach our works were rejected. In subsequent offensive actions, the Air Force broke and shooted enemy mechanized nuclei: numerous vehicles were damaged and destroyed. In the Giarabub area an enemy attack was repelled. The British bombed some of our bases without causing damage.

BULLETIN No. 207 of December 31:
In the Cyrenaic border area, actions by our artillery and fighter aviation by stripping and strafing against groups of enemy tanks and armored personnel carriers that were repelled and damaged, while attempting to get closer to our positions., Distant actions of artillery and bombing aircraft against the Sollum base. In the night between 29 and 30 enemy planes bombed our fields in Cyrenaica without loss or damage.

BULLETIN No. 208 of January 1, 1941
In the Cyrenaic border area, activities of our artillery, which have effectively beaten enemy autocolumns. An enemy attack against our advanced post on the Bardia front has been repelled. In another fight, in the Giarabub area, our troops fled an enemy unit supported by armored personnel carriers. Our aerial assault and hunting formations have carried out repeated actions on concentrations of enemy mechanized vehicles, inflicting significant losses on them.

BULLETIN No. 209 of January 2
In the Cyrenaic border area, artillery and patrols activities on the Bardia front. In the Giarabub area, on the battlefield reported in yesterday's bulletin, we collected weapons, ammunition and trucks abandoned by the enemy. Opposing air raids on our fields of Cyrenaica produced minor damage and no casualties; effective hunting and anti-aircraft reaction; an enemy aircraft was shot down. Our assault and hunting formations bombed and strafed numerous mechanized elements and a reduced enemy. All our appliances have returned.

BULLETIN No. 210 of January 3
In the Cyrenaic border area, our artillery battles mechanized formations and enemy naval vessels. Bombing planes repeatedly attacked an opponent's advanced base and ships off the coast, hitting a cruiser. Other planes bombed and strafed mechanized formations on the Bardia front and in the desert. All our appliances have returned.

BULLETIN No. 212 of January 5
The battle on the Bardia front continued with increasing violence all day yesterday, and is still ongoing. Hunting and assault formations participated by machine-gunning and

breaking enemy troops in various locations, immobilizing and destroying armored vehicles. Despite the heroic behavior of our land and air units, some strong points have fallen into the hands of the enemy. The air force repeatedly bombed enemy naval forces off Bardia and mechanized columns. Opposing air raids on our fields have caused minor damage to personnel and material. During the air battles, our fighter has shot down eight enemy aircraft so far. Three of our aircraft have not returned.

BULLETIN No. 213 of January 6
The battle on the Bardia front continued fiercely yesterday from morning to night Other cornerstones have fallen after a strenuous resistance from our troops, which have inflicted significant losses on the opponent. The aviation continued to work in competition with ground actions. Enemy planes bombed our bases without causing damage. One of our planes has not returned.

BULLETIN No. 214 of January 7th
The last cornerstones that still resisted in Bardia fell towards the evening of the 5th. Our troops have, for 25 days, written sublime pages of daring and inflicted heavy losses on the enemy. Ours were also strong, in materials, in men: deads, wounded, missing. During an enemy raid on Tobruk, two enemy aircraft were shot down by the Royal Navy's anti-aircraft artillery.

BULLETIN No. 215 of January 8
In Cyrenaica, patrols and artillery actions between Bardia and Tobruk. Our planes torpedoed an enemy destroyer near Sollum. Hunting and assault patrols have machine-gunned and broken mechanized adversaries. Numerous incursions were carried out by the enemy air force on various locations in Cyrenaica and on the town of Tripoli, where four dead and about ten injured people complain. An enemy plane was shot down in combat by one of our fighters.

BULLETIN No. 216 of January 9
In Cyrenaica, on the terrestrial front, no major news. Our hunting and assault formation attacked a group of enemy mechanized vehicles destroying several armored personnel carriers. Opposing air raids on Benghazi and Tripoli caused slight material damage and three deaths in Tripoli.

BULLETIN No. 217 of January 10th
(...) In Cyrenaica, artillery shots in the Tobruk area, during which enemy mechanized vehicles were destroyed. Our planes bombed the port of Sollum; an assault and hunting formation sighted and struck a hundred enemy mechanized vehicles heading for Acroma south - west of Tobruk.

BULLETIN No. 218 of 11 January
(...) In Cyrenaica, artillery actions in the Tobruk area and near Giarabub. An assault and hunting formation of ours attacked a formation of tanks and armored cars, destroying several of them; in air combat, a Hurricane type fighter aircraft was shot down. Enemy air raids on Tobruk and in the Benghazi area caused some damage and nine deaths, of which seven were children and four were all Muslims. The crew of an English plane

forced to land was captured.

BULLETIN No. 219 of January 12
(...) In Cyrenaica, artillery and patrol activities. Our aircraft bombed enemy formations near Giarabub. Repeated enemy air attacks on some of our bases in Cyrenaica.

BULLETIN N° 220 of 13 January
On the Greek front, normal patrols and artillery activities. Our aircraft have strafed and broken marching troops and columns of vehicles. In Cyrenaica, artillery activities on the forehead of Tobruk and our swift columns in the desert around Giarabub. An enemy advanced base has been effectively bombed. The enemy air force bombed some places in Cyrenaica without causing casualties.

BULLETIN N° 221 of January 14
(...) In Cyrenaica, activities of our artillery, which inflicted losses to enemy mechanized vehicles on the Tobruk front and actions of patrols and artillery in the Giarabub area. Enemy aerial actions on places on the Cyrenaean coast did not cause casualties.

BULLETIN No. 222 of January 15
(...) In Cirenaica, occasional artillery and patrols in the Tobruk and Giarabub areas: our planes have effectively broken up armored cars and bombed enemy artillery. The enemy made raids on some places in Libya causing some damage to buildings.

BULLETIN No. 223 of January 16
(...) In Cyrenaica, the usual artillery activity on the front of Tobruk and our swift columns in the Giarabub area. Our planes bombed rolling stock, refueling posts and enemy preparations south - east of Tobruk. An enemy aircraft in reconnaissance on Tobruk was shot down by the anti-aircraft defense of the R. Marina.

BULLETIN No. 224 of January 17
(...) In Cyrenaica artillery and patrols.

BULLETIN No. 225 of January 18
(...) In Cyrenaica increased artillery and patrol activities on the Tobruk front. During an enemy air raid, a *Hurricane*-type aircraft was shot down by the anti-aircraft defense of the *R. Marina*. On the Giarabub front, our planes bombed and strafed enemy troops and mechanized vehicles.

BULLETIN No. 226 of January 19
(...) In northern Africa, artillery activities in the Tobruk sector and our motorized patrols in the southern Cyrenaic desert.

BULLETIN No. 227 of January 20
(...) In Cyrenaica actions of artillery and patrols on the fronts of Giarabub and Tobruk. Near Giarabub our planes bombed enemy armoured vehicles with excellent results. The enemy made an air raid on Tobruk: one of his aircraft was shot down by anti-aircraft defense.

BULLETIN No. 228 of January 21
(...) In Cyrenaica, increased gunner activity around Tobruk and enemy air activity on Tobruk Square, causing some damage to the material and none to the staff. Our planes have repeatedly bombed enemy preparations and bases.

BULLETIN No. 229 of January 22
(...) The enemy attacks against the Tobruk stronghold, which had already been completely surrounded and beaten daily by artillery and planes for twenty days, began yesterday morning 21. It was preceded in the night by a naval bombardment lasted until dawn and was sustained during the day by continuous air raids from enemy bombardment. Three Australian Divisions were identified as participants in the attack, reinforced by two heavy artillery regiments, two armored Divisions and a French motorized formation of so-called dissidents. At the end of the day, after fierce fighting, the enemy had managed to penetrate the line of the strongholds of the eastern sector of the fortress.

BULLETIN No. 230 of January 23
(...) The bitter battle between the strongpoints of the Tobruk stronghold continued throughout the day of yesterday. Only in the afternoon did the Australians enter the town of Tobruk where everything had been set on fire and the old ship *San Giorgio* had been blown up with dynamite. In the western sector of the square, some cornerstones still offer strong resistance to enemy attack. The Italian forces concentrated in Tobruk consisted of a single Division plus some Navy units and border guards. The enemy himself is forced to admit that the losses suffered by his five attacking Divisions have been particularly severe. Our air force had bombed concentrations of enemy troops; that opponent made raids on some places in Libya causing some damage.

BULLETIN No. 231 of January 24
(...) In Cyrenaica our air force has severely bombed and strafed mechanized means of the enemy; the opposing air force bombed Derna. In the stronghold of Tobruk, our groups opposed in the west, a fierce resistance throughout the day of yesterday.

BULLETIN No. 232 of January 25
The latest units that in the western sector of Tobruk opposed a desperate resistance to the enemy attack, were overwhelmed yesterday. The forces that were in the stronghold of Tobruk consisted of an Infantry Division, the *Sirte*, a battalion of border guards, a battalion of Black Shirts, crews of sailors and gunboats: a total of about 20 thousand men. These forces resisted the unceasing triple bombing of land, sea and air for 19 days and stood up to the final assault for four days. Our artillery fired to the last bullet and produced large voids in the Australian units. Our losses in men and materials have also been strong. According to a radio communication from the enemy, over two thousand Italian woundeds have been cleared from Tobruk. In the battle of Tobruk which was very hard, according to the same enemy confession, the armed forces of Italy heroically fought. After Tobruk, the battle moved west, where stakes of enemy armored vehicles were repelled by our fire, to which was added the bombing and strafing carried out by our air force; an enemy *Blenheim*-like plane was shot down by our fighter.

BULLETIN No. 233 of January 26
(...) In Cyrenaica, fighting is underway with the effective cooperation of our aviation, which works its best by breaking up and machine-gunning enemy troops and mechanized vehicles. Yesterday our hunt, having reached an enemy formation, shot down four Gloster-type aircraft in flames.

BULLETIN No. 234 of January 27
(...) In Cyrenaica, in lively fighting in the east and south of Derna, our troops inflicted significant losses on enemy armored vehicles. Our air force bombed, shooted and strafed strong mechanized concentrations and artillery. Two British aircraft were shot down by our fighter.

BULLETIN No. 235 of January 28
(...) In Cyrenaica the fighting continues east of Derna. Our troops repelled an enemy column, inflicting losses and capturing prisoners. Our air force dropped small bombs and strafed armored vehicles and enemy infantry. In combat our fighter shot down two Hurricane-type aircraft.

BULLETIN No. 236 of January 29
(...) In Cyrenaica, south of Derna, an attack by an enemy Armored Division was repelled by our troops, which inflicted significant losses on the opponent. Our aerial units have done their utmost by bombing, breaking and machine-guns incessantly armored cores, vehicles and enemy troops. The air assault group has distinguished itself for its tireless and heroic activity.

BULLETIN No. 237 of January 30th
(...) In Cyrenaica, intense activity of artillery, patrols and swift cores, actively assisted by our aviation.

BULLETIN No. 238 of January 31
(...) In Cyrenaica, the Upper Command, in order to avoid circumventing our positions in Derna, ordered the evacuation of the city and moved the troops immediately to the west and south, where our units crushed an attack by motorized Australian troops. Air formations bombed British armoured vehicles. Our fighters shot down two aircrafts. The enemy made raids on a place in Cyrenaica, causing three deaths and some injured; slight material damage.

BULLETIN No. 239 of February 1
(...) In Cyrenaica, our armored units attacked and repelled enemy means south of the Jebel, which were bombed by our air force.

BULLETIN No. 240 of February 2
(...) In Cyrenaica, no news worth mentioning. Our aerial units bombed enemy mechanized cores. Two *Hurricane*-type aircraft were shot down by our fighter. The enemy made raids on our airfields, with damage, but without deads or wondeds.

BULLETIN No. 241 of February 3

(...) In northern Africa, our aircrafts have successfully bombed columns of British mechanized vehicles.

BULLETIN No. 242 of February 4
(...) In northern Africa, intense aviation activity of ours and our adversaries.

BULLETIN No. 243 of February 5
(...) In northern Africa, activities of the opposite aviations. British planes bombed Benghazi.

BULLETIN No. 244 of February 6
(...) In North Africa, our planes strafed and cracked British armoured vehicles.

Ghemines
(Kurt Caesar, 1941. Author's collection).

El Mechili
(Kurt Caesar, 1941. Author's collection)

OPERATIONS IN LIBYA.
WAVELL'S REPORT TO THE WAR CABINET IN LONDON, FEBRUARY 1941.

TO BE KEPT UNDER LOCK AND KEY.

It is requested that special care may be taken to ensure the secrecy of this document.

WAR CABINET.

OPERATIONS IN LIBYA.

Note by the Secretary of State for War.

I CIRCULATE, for the information of my colleagues, the annexed telegram which has been received from the Commander-in-Chief, Middle East, regarding the operations in Libya.

D. M. War Office, S.W. 1, February 16, 1941.

(1/41035)

FOR reasons operational secrecy no previous publicity given activities armoured Division. At your discretion these can now be broadcast.
Success phase operations starting Sidi Barrani and culminating Benghazi has been due in large measure to ascendency moral and material established by armoured Division over enemy from very outset Italian declaration of War.
From word go armoured Division took offensive and, with the exception of period during which they were withdrawn for strategical reasons to allow Italian forces to stretch themselves across frontier to Sidi Barrani, they have consistently attacked. In early days units of armoured Division penetrated and temporarily cleared tracts of hostile territory running into thousands of square miles. Gradually they were pressed back by establishment successive defended localities by forces numerically superior as ten to one employing artillery twenty or thirty to one. Result, this extraordinary moral ascendency evident every stage of operations leading to capture Benghazi. If British armoured units even in small number- appeared to threaten line of retreat, first Italian impulse was to hesitate and then assume defensive instead of trying to break through.
Using different methods of surprise bold use of numerically inferior forces worked time after time. Spectacular finish to this phase epitomises not only dash of its leaders and determination tenacity of troops, but it also speaks volumes for quality and standard of British equipment. For nearly eight months armoured Division has been employed without rest.
Vehicles which had already withstood strain protracted operations in worst possible

conditions sand and heat were able in last dash to make final and protracted burst which completely surprised enemy. Weight for class Italian tanks, many of them newly delivered from manufacturers, proved no match for British products.

Other (? facts) value of long and carefully directed individual and collective training, physical fitness, individual intiative and contribution by workers at home to victories in the field.

Publicity may also be given to activities of long-range desert patrols. Italian garrisons at Kufra and other desert posts provided amongst other duties L. of C. for interchange Italian aircraft between Libya and Italian East Africa.

Kufra also constituted potential threat to Nile Valley soon after declaration war, long-range desert patrols formed under leadership major, now lieut.-colonel. Bagnold with nucleus scattered Englishmen who in peace time made their hobby exploration of Libyan Desert.

Within six weeks of inception, patrols composed picked officers and men New Zealand forces and Royal Armoured Corps started their activities. In conditions of indescribable hardship these patrols constantly scoured desert, shooting up convoys, destroying petrol dumps and generally harassing Italian desert garrisons. Immediate result was cessation of normal supply convoys, increase Italian garrisons and many other comings and goings. Having achieved first object our patrols in concert Free French commenced operations in (? Fed An). Story of our action with French co-operation at Murzuk, our capture of Traghan and other lesser posts has already been told by General Catroux. Original personnel have now been augmented by volunteers from British units and Rhodesians.

In company with French, operations by our long-range desert patrols are now in progress about Kufra. As further tribute to British work-manship, noteworthy that vehicles by these patrols have now covered total distance half a million miles without loss of single vehicle from mechanical breakdown, this is all the more praiseworthy if realised that for obvious reasons patrols unable use recognised tracks and have found their own ways over sand seas, uncharted desert, outcrops of rock and other difficulties previously considered by most seasoned explorers to be totally impassible.

As final note, service of transport drivers throughout all operations in Libya in desert Sudan and Kenya merits special mention. Their work has been magnificent. Undeterred by perpetual sandstorms, by bombing, by shortage of water and other physical difficulties our transport drivers British, from Dominions, India, Cyprus and Cape have never failed to support their comrades in fighting line by delivering their loads at right place and time. Road maintenance of vehicles has been above reproach, courage and devotion to duty admirable.

ITALIAN TANKS' TECHNICAL DATA

CARRO ARMATO LEGGERO L3/ 33 (CV33)

Year of entry into service: 1933
Crew: 2 men
Weight: 3.2 t
Dimensions: length 3.15 m;
width 1.40 m;
height 1.28 m
Engine: petrol, 43 hp power
Speed 42 km / h
Autonomy: 120 km
Armor: front 13.5 mm, side 6 mm
Armament: 1 machine gun Fiat Revelli 14

CARRO LEGGERO L3/35 (CV35)

Year of entry into service: 1935
Crew: 2 men
Weight: 3.2 t
Dimensions: length 3.15 m;
width 1.40 m;
height 1.28 m
Engine: petrol, 43 hp power
Speed 42 km / h
Autonomy: 125 km
Armor: front 15,5 mm, lateral 8,5 mm
Armament: 2 machine guns Fiat 35 or Breda 38.

The flamethrower version was called L35LF .; instead of one of the machine guns, it mounted a flamethrower tube powered by an external tank that could be mounted either on the engine inspection hatch or on a special remover. The modification was carried out on both CV.33 (L33LF) and CV35 hulls.

CARRO MEDIO M 11/39

Year of entry into service: 1939
Crew: 3 men
Weight 11 t approx
Dimensions: length 4.85 m;
width 2.18 m;
height 2.11
Engine: Diesel, 105 hp power
Speed: 32km / h
Autonomy: 210 km on the road, 12 hours off road
Armor: front 30 mm, lateral 14.5 mm
Armament: 1 37 mm gun, 2 machine guns cal. 8 Breda 38; Radio equipment: intercom for internal communications, 1 Marelli RF 1 CA radio complex

CARRO MEDIO M 13/40

Year of entry into service: 1940
Crew: 4 men
Weight approx. 14 t
Dimensions: length 4.91 m;
width 2.28 m;
height 2.37
Engine: Diesel, power 125 hp
Speed: 32km / h, off-road 15km / h
Autonomy: 200 km on the road, 12 hours off road
Armor: front 30 mm, side 25 mm
Armament: 1 semi-automatic 47/32 gun, 3 machine guns cal. 8 Breda 38.

BIBLIOGRAPHY

AAVV 1954, *The Mediterranean and the Middle East, I, The Early Successes against Italy (to May 1941), History of the Second World War:* United Kingdom Military Series, HMSO, London.

J. Baynes, 1989, *The Forgotten Victor: General Sir Richard O'Connor, KT, GCB, DSO, MC* , Potomack Books, Lincoln.

F. Bandini 1980, *Gli Italiani in Africa*, Mondadori, Milano.

P. Baroni 2001, *Generali nella polvere. Perche abbiamo perduto in Africa Settentrionale (giugno 1940 - febbraio 1941).* Settimo Sigillo, Roma.

C. Barnett 1982 2nd, *The Desert Generals*, Indiana University Press, Bloomington.

M. Berchtold 2017, *Flying to Victory. Raymond Collishaw and the Western Desert campaign 1940- 1941*, University of Oklahoma Press, Norman.

J. Bierwirth 2013, *Beda Fomm. An Operational Analysis*, Pickle Partners Publ., East Lansing.

A.Biagini, F. Frattolillo 1988, *Diario Storico del Comando Supremo (1.9.1940 - 31.12.1940)*, II, USSME, Roma.

A. Bongioanni 1996, *Battaglie nel deserto. da Sidi- el- Barrani a El Alamein*, Mursia, Milano.

A. Borgiotti, C. Gori 1972, *Guerra aerea in Africa Settentrionale 1940- 1941*, Stem Mucchi, Modena.

O. Bovio 1999, *In alto la bandiera. Storia del Regio Esercito*, Bastogi, Foggia.

G. Bucciante 1989, *I generali della dittatura*, Mondadori, Milano.

R. Canosa 2005, *Graziani. Il Maresciallo d'Italia dalla guerra d'Etiopia alla Repubblica di Salò*, Mondadori, Milano.

U. Cavallero 1984, *Diario 1940- 1943* (a cura di G. Bucciante), Ciarrapico, Roma.

G. Cecini 2016, *I generali di Mussolini*, Newton Compton, Roma.

L. Ceva 1982, *Africa settentrionale 1940- 1943*, Bonacci, Roma.

H. R. Christie 1999, *Fallen Eagles: the Italian 10th Army in the opening campaign in the western desert, June 1940 - December 1940,* U.S. Army Command and General Staff College, Fort Leavenworth.

G. Ciano 1990, *Diario 1937- 1943* (a cura di R. De Felice), Rizzoli, Milano.

J. Connell 1964, *Wavell. Scholar and Soldier*, Collins, London.

A. Cova 1987, *Graziani. Un generale per il regime*, Newton Compton, Roma.

C. De Biase 1969, *L'Aquila d'oro. Storia dello Stato Maggiore Italiano (1861- 1945)*, Il Borghese, Milano.

R. De Felice 1990, *Mussolini l'alleato. 1. L'Italia in guerra 1940-43. 1. Dalla guerra "breve" alla guerra lunga*, Einaudi, Torino.

G. Forty 1990, *The First Victory: General O'Connor's Desert Triumph, Dec. 1940- Feb. 1941*, Nutshells publ., Turnbridge Wells.

J. Fest 1973, *Hitler. Eine Biographie*, Propyläen Verlag, Frankfurt/m, Berlin, Wien (tr. it. Rizzoli, Milano 1974)

D. Fraser 1993, *Knight's Cross. The Life of Feldmarschall Erwin Rommel*, Harper-Collins, London.

J. Gooch 2007, *Mussolini and His Generals: The Armed Forces and Fascist Foreign Policy, 1922–1940*. (Cambridge Military Histories.), Cambridge University Press, New York.

J. Gooch 2020, *Mussolini's War: Fascist Italy from Triumph to Collapse, 1935-1943*, Allen Lane, London.

R. Graziani 1947, *Ho difeso la Patria*, Garzanti, Milano.

R. Graziani 1948, *Africa Settentrionale 1940- 1941*, Danesi, Roma.

J. Greene 1990, *Mare Nostrum. The War in the Mediterranean*, Greene, Watsonville.

J. Greene, A. Massignani 1994, *Rommel's North Africa Campaign*, Da Capo, New York.

G. B. Guerri 1998, *Italo Balbo*, Mondadori, Milano.

S. Jowett 2000, *The Italian Army 1940- 1945 [2] Africa 1940- 43*, Osprey, Oxford.

M. Knox, *Mussolini Unleashed, 1939–1941: Politics and Strategy in Fascist Italy's Last War*, Cambridge University Press, Cambridge 1982

J. Keegan (editor), *Churchill's Generals*, Grove Weidenfeld, New York, 1991.

J. Latimer, J. Laurier 2000, *Operation Compass 1940. Wavell's whirlwind offensive*, Osprey, Oxford.

K. Macksey, B. Pitt 1971, *Beda Fomm: The Classic Victory*, Ballantine Books,New York.

G. Mayda 1992, *Graziani l'Africano. Da Neghelli a Salò*, La Nuova Italia Editrice, Firenze.

P. Maravigna 1949, *Come abbiamo perduto la guerra in Africa*, Tosi, Roma.

A. Mollo 1981, *The Armed Forces of World War II*, London (tr. it. Ist. Geogr. De Agostini, Novara 1982).

M. Montanari 1985, *Le operazioni in Africa Settentrionale. I. Sidi el Barrani (Giugno 1940- Febbraio 1941)*, USSME, Roma.

M. Patricelli 2016, *L'Italia delle sconfitte: da Custoza alla ritirata di Russia*, Laterza, Roma- Bari.

B. Perret 1979, *Armour in Battle: Wavell Offensive*, Ian Allan, London.

B. Pitt, 1980,*The Crucible of War: Wavell's Command*. I, Johnatan Cape, London.

D.Quirico 2002, *Squadrone bianco. Storia delle truppe coloniali italiane*, Mondadori, Milano.

H. E. Raugh jr 1993,*Wavell in the Middle East: a Study in Generalship*, Brassey's, London.

P. Romeo di Colloredo 2009, *I Pilastri del Romano Impero, Le Camicie Nere in Africa Orientale, 1935-1936*, Italia storica, Genova.

P. Romeo di Colloredo 2017, *Camicia Nera! Storia militare della Milizia Volontaria per la Sicurezza nazionale dalle origini al 25 luglio*, Soldiershop, Bergamo.

P. Romeo di Colloredo 2019, *Da Sidi el Barrani a Beda Fomm 1940- 1941. La Caporetto di Mussolini*, .

P. Romeo di Colloredo 2019[a], *Per vincere ci vogliono i leoni... I fronti dimenticati delle camicie nere, 1939- 1940*, Soldiershop, Bergamo

G. Rochat 2006, *Le guerre italiane 1935-1943. Dall'impero d'Etiopia alla disfatta*, Einaudi, Torino.

H. Rowan-Robinson 1942, *Wavell in the Middle East*, London.

A. Santangelo 2012, *Operazione Compass, la Caporetto del deserto*, Salerno, Roma.

N. Smart, 2005, *Biographical Dictionary of British Generals of the Second World War*, Pen & Sword, Barnsley.

J. J. T. Sweet 2006, *Iron Arm: the Mechanization of Mussolini's Army, 1920- 1940*, Stackpole, Mechanicsburg.
R. Tyre 1999, *Mussolini's Afrika Korps. The Italian Army in North Africa 1940-1943,* Europa Books, New York
M. Tobino 2011, *Il deserto della Libia*, nuova ed. Mondadori, Milano..
Ufficio storico dello Stato maggiore dell'Esercito 1972, *La prima offensiva britannica in Africa settentrionale*, USSME, Roma.
I. W. Walker 2003, *Iron Hulls, Iron Hearts: Mussolini's Elite Armoured Divisions in North Africa*, Crowood, Marlborough.
W. S.Zapotoczny, Jr. 2018, *The Italian Army in North Africa: A Poor Fighting Force or Doomed by Circumstance,* Fonthill, Stroud.

El Mechili's Fort
(drawing by Kurt Caesar. Author's collection.)

STORIA

www.ingramcontent.com/pod-product-compliance
Lightning Source LLC
LaVergne TN
LVHW081542070526
838199LV00057B/3752